EXAMINATIONS IN CIVIL TRIALS

THE COMPLETE YOUNG ADVOCATES SERIES

Discovery Techniques: A Practical Guide to the Discovery Process

The Art of the Interview: How Lawyers Talk With Clients

Legal Writing: Mastering Clarity and Precision

The Civil Courtroom: Professionalism to Build Rapport

Mediation for Civil Litigators: Issues and Solutions

Case Analysis: The Critical Path to Persuasion

EXAMINATIONS IN CIVIL TRIALS

the formula for success

JOHN HOLLANDER

Examinations in Civil Trials: The Formula for Success

Published in 2015 by
Irwin Law Inc
Suite 206, 14 Duncan Street
Toronto, ON M5H 3G8
www.irwinlaw.com

ISBN: 978-1-55221-380-3 e-book ISBN: 978-1-55221-381-0

Library and Archives Canada Cataloguing in Publication

Hollander, John, 1951–, author
Examinations in civil trials : the formula for success / John Hollander.

(Young advocates series)
Includes index.
Issued in print and electronic formats.
ISBN 978-1-55221-380-3 (pbk.).—978-1-55221-381-0 (pdf)

1. Examination of witnesses. I. Title. II. Series: Hollander, John, 1951–. Young advocates series.

K2271.H64 2015 347'.075 C2015-902055-7
C2015-902056-5

The publisher acknowledges the financial support of the Government of Canada through the Canada Book Fund for its publishing activities.

We acknowledge the assistance of the OMDC Book Fund, an initiative of the Ontario Media Development Corporation.

Printed and bound by CPI Group (UK) Ltd, Croydon, CR0 4YY
1 2 3 4 5 19 18 17 16 15

About the Young Advocates Series

WHAT IS THERE to bridge the gap between law school and law practice? It used to be that experience in both transactions and courtrooms taught junior lawyers everything that law school missed. Today, the legal system has become so complex that trials are few and far between, and those that occur take weeks or months, not days. Transactions are also far more complex than they once were. It always seems that so much is at stake — all the time.

The result of all this complexity is that senior lawyers do not generally assign significant responsibility to their juniors. They delegate tasks, not files. A junior litigator or transactions lawyer simply does not learn as much or as well when playing a subordinate role when compared to having full responsibility for a file.

Traditionally, law schools teach legal theory and legal analysis. Increasingly, however, they have started to teach some students entry-level practicalities, from trial advocacy to negotiation to alternative dispute resolution. They teach to enable students to succeed in law school, but not to succeed in law practice. This may come in the future, but law schools are a long way from accomplishing that today.

This creates a need for practical advice, in the form of concise, practical handbooks, for each of the many subjects that junior lawyers require to get through their days. This series, which has emerged from the Ottawa-based Advocacy Club, seeks to fill that need. Founded in 2007, the Club trains junior advocates how to conduct interviews and prepare for and to conduct examinations. In the process, they learn collegiality, civility, and modern techniques that help to make them professionals.

A word about what these handbooks are and are not. The handbooks are not comprehensive replacements for legal education. They do not contain legal citations or war stories from real or imagined victories in a glorious past. They do contain a great many tips and techniques that permit the thoughtful junior lawyer to develop and advance the skills essential to success in the profession.

The series author, John Hollander, founded the Advocacy Club and serves as a trainer and mentor to junior litigators in Ottawa. Called to the Bar of Ontario in 1978, John has been a civil litigator throughout his legal career. He learned his lessons the hard way, through trial and error, and with guidance from his seniors and judges. He has considered the lessons that junior lawyers must learn to succeed, and he presents them in a thought-provoking manner that aims to engage the reader.

Contents

Examinations in Civil Trials: Use of This Handbook

LITIGATORS HAVE SEVERAL tools to persuade decision makers. To be effective, lawyers should present a consistent face to their audiences. This was the central message in the Young Advocates Series's other handbooks, such as *Legal Writing*[1] and *Case Analysis*.[2]

Examinations (both direct and cross) are applications of case analysis principles. Before counsel asks a question, there has to be a thorough analysis:

- What goals are there to accomplish?
- Why ask any questions at all?
- Why ask this particular question?
- How will the answer lead to other questions?
- What are the choices?
- What are the risks?

---

1 John Hollander, *Legal Writing: Mastering Clarity and Persuasion* (Toronto: Irwin Law, 2013), online: www.irwinlaw.com/titles/legal-writing.

2 John Hollander, *Case Analysis: The Critical Path to Persuasion* (Toronto: Irwin Law, 2014), online: www.irwinlaw.com/titles/case-analysis.

This handbook presents several situations that confront examiners both when they prepare to face a witness and when the witness takes the stand. Each situation presents issues and solutions. Each confronts the reader with the judgment calls that are essential to the litigator's profession.

Structure

THERE ARE SIX chapters that make up this handbook:

1. The first chapter introduces the reader to techniques necessary for preparation for examinations.
2. This chapter lays out techniques that are common to various forms of examination: out-of-court examination, direct examination, or cross-examination.
3. This chapter introduces the trial judge (or chair of a tribunal). While not the only audience, the advocate usually presents evidence to persuade a judge. This chapter presents several techniques to assist the lawyer in accomplishing that goal.
4. This chapter discusses techniques that are primarily used in direct examinations (often referred to as examinations-in-chief), where counsel should not lead the witness.
5. This chapter presents techniques that are primarily used in cross-examinations.
6. The final chapter discusses redirect examinations.

Practising what I preach, this handbook is the result of an outline. The sequence of the chapters makes sense to me, but readers should flip between chapters in any order that makes sense to them. Perhaps a reader has a case coming up, and one or two chapters seem to apply. There is no need to read every chapter up to the one in question. For the most part, they do not build on each other. There are many ideas expressed here, but the central thesis is expressed in "The 'Five-and-Out' Formula" and "Short Questions, Simple Language," below in Chapter 1.

Terminology

"CHIEF" AND "DIRECT examination" are used interchangeably, to avoid annoying repetition. The word "examiner" is used to mean the lawyer who asks questions in either direct examination or cross-examination. The phrases "direct examiner" and "cross-examiner" are used with respect to those specific situations. The words "lawyer," "counsel," "litigator," and "advocate" are used interchangeably, to avoid repetition. The author avoids the use of gender throughout the series. This leads to the use of the passive voice or plurals, which may seem convoluted, but it is all in support of a good cause.

Case Studies

IN MANY CHAPTERS, there is a case study. This is an invented fact situation used to prompt an exercise. Each exercise demonstrates the principles discussed in the chapter, and each offers the reader the chance to practise what the handbook preaches. Each case study contains a "solution," which is an expression of how an advocate might tackle the exercise. It is not intended to be perfect.

In some cases, it may be controversial. It is just a demonstration. Think of these case studies as chess problems in the local newspaper: "White queen to king's rook 4. Mate in 4 moves."

Conclusion

MANY IDEAS APPEAR to be put forward as principles. They are really guidelines. Each lawyer has to act in accordance with the rules of professional conduct and the rules of the courts. Not all principles work in every case. Lawyers have to figure out what works for them, as stressed in the section "Know Yourself as a Cross-examiner," below in Chapter 5.

Acknowledgements

THIS HANDBOOK IS part of the Young Advocates Series. Irwin Law demonstrated the vision to support a series of practical handbooks aimed at lawyers looking to develop skills largely ignored by law schools and bar associations, and at a price within reach of young lawyers still saddled with student loans. In particular, Irwin Law's Alisa Posesorski and John Sawicki have been instrumental in turning this vision into reality.

Finally, the energy, enthusiasm, and talent of the members of the Advocacy Club and my classes at the University of Ottawa's Common Law Section deserve acknowledgement. They have endured the constant trial and error that goes into teaching in a novel method. Some of the exercises were less than wonderful, but the Club members met each challenge with good cheer, collegiality, and imagination.

How to Teach Courtroom Examination Techniques

WHAT IS THE value of a good war story? Experienced lawyers love to tell them, after work hours, with a glass of beer. Young lawyers love to listen to them. Or do they?

In the English system of legal training, barristers had to attend dinners at their Inn of Court to qualify for the bar. This medieval tradition arose in the seventeenth century or earlier and was scrapped only recently. In effect, this practice institutionalized the tradition of war stories. Is that all there is to learning the tricks of the litigation trade? The fact is that two components are essential to succeed in any trade: technique and practice, and neither of these components can be taught by war stories. That wonderful question counsel used to elicit just the right answer at just the right moment? That will never recur. If it does, the young litigator will recognize the opportunity only after having missed it.

This is the seventh handbook in the Young Advocates Series. It deals with the rough and tumble of examinations that occur during civil trials, both direct and cross. This handbook, indeed the entire Young Advocates Series, provides practical techniques for the novice litigator.

For those counsel with more experience, it may offer alternatives to practices developed over years. Generally speaking, litigators can use the techniques in cases involving both trial court and administrative tribunal disputes. Granted, the practices of a particular courtroom or administrative tribunal may differ from one to the next. Nevertheless, the techniques discussed in this handbook are universal in their application. They arise from a commonsense approach to how people present and absorb information.

Junior litigators need several skills to work effectively, one of which is the ability to examine witnesses. This skill does not exist in a vacuum, in isolation — quite the contrary. Before they open their mouths, litigators should know what they want to say and why they want to say it. This involves case analysis. The reader is referred to *Case Analysis* in this series.

With the emergence of alternative dispute resolution (ADR) and with the increase in the cost of trials, junior litigators rarely get the chance to practise the skills they acquire (or should acquire) in law school. How do they acquire the real-time skills necessary for their trade except from experience? Often, from bitter experience. This handbook provides some of the answers to questions that junior litigators should ask. If readers can learn a tip or two from each chapter, then this will be a huge advance in their professional development.

chapter one

Preparation for Examinations

THERE ARE SEVERAL techniques generally common to the examinations that litigators conduct. This chapter of the handbook deals with what examiners must consider before they enter the courtroom.

Essentially, litigators have to think before they open their mouth. The thought process is dealt with at length in the Young Advocates Series's *Case Analysis* and *Discovery Techniques*[1] handbooks. Preparation is a work in progress, as the more the lawyer learns and thinks, the more the lawyer can fine-tune questions to accomplish the best results. There are several preparation techniques that the lawyer should learn and master, some of which are canvassed in this chapter. There is some overlap with the following chapters that deal with specific examinations.

Examiners must consider their strategy and tactics before they ask questions of witnesses. Strategy is necessary to identify and set the goals in the bigger picture, the case. Tactics are necessary to arrange the right questions

1 John Hollander, *Discovery Techniques: A Practical Guide to the Discovery Process in Civil Actions* (Toronto: Irwin Law, 2013), online: www.irwinlaw.com/titles/discovery-techniques.

to accomplish those goals. Preparation includes both the lawyer and the witness (in direct examinations). This is a three-step process:

1. The lawyer prepares to see the witness.
2. The lawyer then prepares the witness.
3. Finally, the lawyer prepares for the examination.

This chapter addresses two subjects: how to consider the case (the "big picture") and the examination (the "little picture") and then how to approach trial examinations in general.

Case Analysis

BEFORE CONDUCTING AN examination, the examiner should know what is to be accomplished and at what risk. This subject is reviewed at length in the sixth handbook of this series, *Case Analysis*. Case analysis consists of six discrete steps:

1. Articulate the issue as succinctly as possible. This should be performed in a neutral fashion that is beyond controversy. The issue can be general (the whole case) or specific (liability, damages, or a specific defence).
2. Identify all of the necessary elements to encompass the case from start to finish. Again, these should be expressed as succinctly as possible. Also, they should be expressed in a neutral fashion that all parties could accept. In this step, the analyst should remove all elements that are not essential to get the analysis from beginning to end.

3. Restate the issue from the point of view of the client of the analyst. The issue should now consist of a few words that bring to mind some emotional reaction. The issue could be phrased in the form of an advertising jingle or commonly used phrase or idiom.
4. Restate all of the necessary elements so that they reflect the position of the analyst's client. Controversy is quite acceptable at this stage. The purpose of the restatement will be to encourage the analyst to determine whether there exists appropriate proof or evidence to establish the spin. The neutral form ("Whether the conduct was excessive") becomes adversarial ("This is a case of abuse").
5. The last two steps require that the analyst think outside the box. Consider the case from the perspective of the opposing party. Restate the issue from the point of view of the opposition, complete with succinct and emotional rephrasing.
6. Restate all of the necessary elements so that they reflect the position of the opposition. Again, the purpose is to encourage the analyst to determine whether the other side has a better story. If so, the analyst should take steps to improve the client's position or else make the best settlement possible.

Why is this necessary in examinations?

THIS IS NECESSARY in examinations because lawyers do not create the story. Witnesses do. Lawyers should ensure that each witness testifies in support of one or more elements. Those witnesses will support the spin that the lawyers identify as being necessary in the fourth step of case analysis. As part of the preparation for cross-examination, those witnesses should be confronted with the questions that arise from the analysis engaged in at the sixth step. Only with this careful preparation will witnesses be ready.

But what about counsel? Preparation of witnesses is itself a three-stage process:

1. Lawyers prepare themselves to discuss the case with the witnesses.
2. Lawyers then prepare the witnesses to be examined. This preparation stage includes the lawyers' asking the hard questions that the witnesses must face for the lawyers' case to succeed.
3. Finally, lawyers prepare themselves to conduct the examination. By this time, they should be armed with a full understanding of what the witnesses will contribute to the stories told by the parties.

What does the lawyer do with this?

CASE ANALYSIS INFORMS the outlines that lawyers prepare for their examinations. While the outline may not mirror the case analysis, it should cover the elements that are necessary to succeed.

The outline should also cover those facts that are essential to the back story that will influence the court in respect of the outcome. Parties do not come to court without history; they have backgrounds, personal attributes, families, occupations, education, and other factors that make them more or less sympathetic. These factors cannot be disregarded by lawyers as they present the evidence. Lawyers routinely seek to tip the scales in favour of their clients through the introduction of evidence that shows their clients in the best light. It is unfortunate that judges, arbitrators, and tribunal chairs are often influenced by extraneous facts. This is the back story. Courts may view certain parties with greater sympathy than others. This sympathy often comes from the back story.

Both direct examinations and cross-examinations seek to portray the witnesses and parties in the best or worst light, which may be accomplished by polishing or tarnishing the credibility of the witness who is testifying.

Conclusion

WHEN LAWYERS EXAMINE witnesses, they must have a purpose in mind. This purpose must accomplish something necessary from the case analysis. Otherwise, there is little merit to having the witness testify at all.

Outlines of Examinations

LAWYERS PREPARE FOR examinations with an outline. Before this, they must consider what they want to accomplish. This should start with the broad strokes, which would include topics with several sub-headings.

Why bother with outlines?

LOOK AT THE advantages of outlines:

1. Most lawyers think in a linear progression, and outlines promote this.
2. Each subject should have a distinct headline. The headline should represent the subject description that

is listed in the outline. This handbook places great importance on headlines.

3. Thoroughness requires that the lawyer consider both the beginning and the end and everything in between. Outlines promote this as well.
4. One of the benefits of headlines is that the author can move any section higher or lower, as the thought process dictates. The topic heading may change its position in the outline from that of a major topic with subtopics to a subtopic on its own. This can occur during the examination itself, should the situation warrant.
5. Outlines can be reviewed easily by a second set of eyes. Consider the case of the junior associate who must submit an outline of an examination to a senior partner before proceeding with the examination. The senior partner can make suggestions regarding areas that have been missed or priorities that should be rearranged. Outlines make this possible.
6. Before the effort is made to flesh out the content of each of the subject areas, it is helpful for lawyers to consider the overall picture, which is what an outline represents.

This is where good case analysis shows its value. As discussed, case analysis should inform all of the examinations that lawyers undertake. Case analysis can, all by itself, provide the initial outline of any examination:

- What does the lawyer have to accomplish with this witness?

- Beyond that, what does the lawyer want to accomplish?
- In what areas must a lawyer inoculate the witness to avoid effective cross-examination?

This is not to say that case analysis is the only step in preparation for examinations. Lawyers must take into account the witnesses as people. This consideration includes the witnesses' ability to recall, to articulate, and to perform under pressure, as well as covering the back story, facts, or attributes that make the testimony more (or less) compelling.

Much of this can be determined at witness interviews that precede the direct examinations. Indeed, this explains why a lawyer's preparation for direct examinations is a three-part process:

1. BEFORE THE INTERVIEW: The lawyer has to know what to say to the witness. There must be a plan of action to get the most benefit from the interview, both to help the witness and, ultimately, to help the lawyer prepare.
2. THE INTERVIEW ITSELF: This is the real-time preparation where the lawyer and the witness form a team.
3. AFTER THE INTERVIEW BUT BEFORE THE EXAMINATION: Lawyers must take into account how the witness will perform before laying out the final outline of the examination.

What does the outline look like?

IN THE CASE of direct examinations, most outlines begin with the identification and relevant biography of the witness. In cross-examination, the witness has usually testified already in chief, which means that there is no need to introduce the witness. The biography portion of an examination serves two purposes:

1. In direct examination, it introduces the witness to the court. In cross, it shows that the witness has blemishes that impact credibility.
2. In direct examination, it puts the witness at ease with the rhythm of any examination. It will help the witness to get used to speaking in an open courtroom, which can be a highly stressful situation, and in cross, it can unsettle the witness. Think of this from the perspective of the witness: alone, in a chair in a strange place, facing questions from serious professionals whom the witness does not know or trust — all overseen by a stern judge, who sits on a raised platform.

The most important component of the examination will be the testimony that supports the elements of the examiner's case analysis. Of secondary importance, there may be some effort to detract from the elements of the case analysis of opposing counsel, which is a major reason why lawyers should also conduct the analysis from the viewpoint of the opposition. On some occasions, the only reason that a witness will testify for one party is to detract from the case of the opposing party. Consider the example of the expert who conducts a "paper review," the sole purpose of which is to attack the findings of the opposition's expert.

In preparing the outline for either the direct examination or the cross-examination, the lawyer should consider each of the elements that will be under consideration. How can the lawyer best establish (or attack) that element? How can this witness communicate that evidence? In direct examination, the witness has to speak the words that will make or break the element. In cross-examination, it is usual for the lawyer to use leading questions to accomplish that goal. The witness should respond only with a monosyllabic "yes" or "no." Lawyers should be very careful not to give the witness an opportunity to give a long answer in cross-examination and should anticipate that the witness is usually not inclined to help the case of the cross-examiner.

How to finish

IT HAS OFTEN been said that lawyers should finish on a high note. While this is a guideline, it cannot be a rule. It is rare that a lawyer can so control the testimony of a witness that the results can be determined in advance with precision. Examinations are unlike choreographed dance routines.

In any event, the outline can put the witness in a position where the testimony will end with a good point. Most often, the high note of the examination occurs at some other moment during the examination. Lawyers should use the outline to arrange the examination to make sense to the audience. Dramatic impact at the end is much less important than successful communication.

And the point is . . .

CONCLUSIONS (REFERRED TO in this handbook as "punchlines") can be considered and prepared in the outline. For the author to record the punchline for each section — the phrase that summarizes the point that the examiner wants to make with the questions — is an excellent practice for outlines. It may or may not be spoken out loud during the examination. In cross, it rarely is spoken during the examination itself.

The outline could state: "The point is . . . ."

When it comes time to describe what was accomplished in the examination (direct or cross), the examiner can identify it quickly. When reviewing the outline to determine what remains to be accomplished, the examiner will know from checkmarks beside the recorded conclusion phrases what has already been accomplished. When preparing closing argument, the lawyer can recite with confidence the points made during the trial.

In cross-examinations, much depends upon what comes out in the direct examination. Lawyers frequently abandon much of their prepared outline based on what was established by the direct examination. Even in this case, lawyers should have a final subject to canvas at the conclusion of cross-examination to make it possible to end on a high note.

As the cross-examination approaches its termination, lawyers should look for a suitable point on which to conclude, and if a sequence of questions has attained an important objective, it may be a good time to sit down. There is always the risk that the next line of questions will leave the examiner's case worse off.

Conclusion

OUTLINES CAN BE of great help to lawyers in both the planning and the implementation stages of examination. They represent the organization of what will be accomplished, they can be tested with second opinions and input from others, they can be reconsidered, and they can be completely amended to suit the circumstances as they develop during the trial. During the examination, they can serve as a checklist for what has been accomplished so far.

Ideally, a combination of case analysis and outlines will result in the closing argument. This may be the ideal, but it may not happen. The best-laid plans rarely survive the first encounter with the opposition.

CASE STUDY

IN A CASE involving occupier's liability where a visitor tripped and fell, the janitor will testify that the lights in the windowless basement had been replaced as part of regular maintenance. The bulbs used were 60-watt bulbs, substituted for the previous 100-watt bulbs to save energy costs. The plaintiff's theory is that poor lighting led to the accident.

Prepare the outline of a direct examination and then prepare the outline of a cross-examination designed to make these two points:

1. The purpose of the replacement bulbs was to save money, not to protect visitors.
2. There was no other light source in the basement.

Solution

Direct examination outline

- Biography of the witness (this witness is knowledgeable about maintenance)
  - » Employment
  - » Training
  - » Experience
  - » Duties
- History of the maintenance in the building and basement (the landlord was diligent)
  - » Changing of the lights
  - » Condition of the basement
  - » Inspections conducted
- This accident (there is no evidence to link poor maintenance to this accident)
  - » No personal knowledge
  - » No complaints otherwise
  - » Inspection after the accident
  - » Condition of the lighting
  - » Safety of the basement
- Inoculation (switching bulbs was a good idea)
  - » Cost of electricity and safety

Cross-examination outline

HEADLINE. Replacement of the lights

- You changed the lights.
- To save money.
- You did not consult a safety expert.

PUNCHLINE. [UNSPOKEN] You did not care about safety, only money.

HEADLINE. Light sources in the basement

- The accident occurred in the basement.
- Below grade.
- The only access was the staircase.
- Several yards from where the plaintiff tripped.
- There were no windows at that level.
- (Optional: The light bulbs were the only source of light there.)

PUNCHLINE. [UNSPOKEN] Visitors had to rely on these light bulbs for safety.

The "Five-and-Out" Formula

THE BEST WAY to assess the likely success of an examination is the degree to which it can accomplish the intended results. This requires two components: careful preparation and implementation. Luck plays a part, but lawyers should not count on good fortune to win the day.

According to the case analysis prepared, what should counsel accomplish with the witness? What points will support the case analysis or attack that of the opposition? The mark of successful preparation is that those points are made by following the outline. Implementation is another matter altogether. How can the lawyer ask just the right questions in just the right manner to have the witness accomplish the desired result?

The method that this handbook preaches is called "five-and-out." There is no magic to the number five. It is a conceptual amount of time, space, and information that is short enough to connect the beginning of an idea to the end. Effectively, it is one sound bite of information. Here is the formula:

1. Identify the subject in the form of a headline. This may come from the case analysis element or the outline label. It should not be controversial. The headline is not a question, just an introduction.
2. Lay out several (four or five) questions that allow the witness's testimony to accomplish the intended result. In cross-examination, each of these questions should be leading in nature and elicit a "yes" or "no." During direct examination, the witness should be presented with open questions.
3. In both cases, direct and cross, the examiner should not make a summary statement of what was accomplished. It should have been accomplished by the witness's words during the direct and by the text of the questions in the cross.

With that, the lawyer then proceeds to the next subject, or headline; this results in an examination that consists of many headlines, each followed by a few questions. In both direct examination and cross-examination, this formula permits the judge to follow what the lawyer is accomplishing through the testimony of the witness.

Criminal defence counsel may object to the use of this formula:

- They believe that a witness who knows about the subject matter before the question is asked is one who is attentive to avoid traps. This objection is aimed at the use of headlines.

- As a second objection, criminal defence counsel want to exploit any progress that they appear to make. They feel that a new headline interrupts the flow and that it detracts from the momentum being achieved. This objection is aimed at the "five" part.

Both of these points are real and have merit in the criminal law context. In that world, counsel can accumulate a great deal of experience fairly soon in their careers. They can switch from outline to gut instinct without loss of performance. Consider the civil case, where junior lawyers get only occasional trial experience. The modern rules that compel alternative dispute resolution (ADR) serve to prevent most junior lawyers from gaining the experience of their colleagues in criminal law.

In answer to the first objection, headlines can be framed in a way that the witness does not know what point the cross-examiner wants to make. Headlines perform the same role in examinations as they do in a newspaper. They inform everybody in the courtroom about just what is under discussion. As an example, consider questions that are designed to elicit testimony concerning the barn at the northeast corner of the farm property. An example of a headline is "I will now ask about the barn at the northeast corner." This precedes a few questions about that barn. Momentum of a cross-examination would be impaired if, the headline having been omitted, the witness interrupted with the question, "What barn is that?" Even more destructive would be for the judge to agree with the witness: "Yes, indeed. What barn?"

The answer to the second objection is more directed to the audience. How can a trial judge appreciate the importance of a successful barrage of cross-examination if the answers come too quickly to write down? Judges do not want to order transcripts just so they can follow a line of questions. The steady rhythm of headline, five questions and answers, point made, next headline (etc.) allows the judge to follow each of the milestones being accomplished. The examiner then uses a pause to allow the judge to catch up where necessary. The use of pauses is discussed elsewhere in this handbook.

The idea of this formula is for the lawyer to implement the outline through a series of questions, each following the form of the outline. In the ideal situation, the notes of the judge will exactly reflect the notes of the outline. It is helpful for the lawyer to record some notes as to what result is intended from each headline. This is the punchline, described in "Outlines of Examinations," above. At trial, the lawyer can mark each headline with a checkmark to signal "Mission accomplished." Take, as an example, an outline point to suggest questions to elicit testimony that a car was proceeding eastbound on the highway as it approached the intersection. The headline might read "We will now discuss what you saw as you approached the intersection." The purpose of the questions is to establish that the witness was or was not paying attention. That would be the note that the lawyer will make beside the questions relating to the five-and-out: "The witness was [or was not] paying attention."

Conclusion

THIS HANDBOOK WILL discuss at much greater length how to implement the five-and-out method in both direct examinations and cross-examinations. However, the purpose of this explanation is to identify that it belongs in all facets of a trial. Consider that it can be equally effective in opening addresses, closing arguments, and even submissions during objections and motions in the course of the trial. Start with the headline, lay out the position in a few points, and then move on to the next. Sound simple? It could well belong in any presentation or in legal writing. For the purpose of this handbook, it clearly belongs in examinations.

CASE STUDY

IN AN INJURY case, the shopper slipped in a puddle formed by melted ice that fell from a produce counter. The direct examiner wants to establish that the shopper slipped in the water. The cross-examiner wants to establish that the shopper should have seen and avoided the danger posed by that water.

Create a headline and a few questions (open in direct, leading in cross) to make the points.

Solution

Direct examination

HEADLINE. Let's discuss what happened at the produce counter.

Q. Why did you go there?

Q. What did you see on the floor before you reached the counter?
Q. What happened when you arrived?
Q. What made you slip?
Q. When did you first notice that it was wet?
PUNCHLINE. [UNSPOKEN] You fell where it was dangerous.

Cross-examination

HEADLINE. Let's discuss what you did at the produce counter.
Q. You walked up to the counter, correct?
Q. You said you slipped in water, correct?
Q. There was nothing to block your vision of the floor, correct?

HEADLINE. Let's discuss what you did not do at the produce counter.
Q. You did not look at the floor, correct?
Q. Where you were walking, correct?
Q. Where you later saw the water, correct?
Q. Which was visible, correct?
Q. Plainly visible, correct?
PUNCHLINE. [UNSPOKEN] You should have noticed.

Short Questions, Simple Language

I TEACH THE techniques described in this series of handbooks to law school students. In the trial advocacy class, English is not the first language for some students. Because the class is experiential in nature (drills), there is no place for them to hide even if they wanted to. The English-as-a-second-language students are confronted with the same problems as all other law students. How do they ask the questions? How do they get the points across? How do they organize their thoughts to the best effect? Then add the translation issue, as they convert their native language thoughts into English actions. The result can be emotionless and ineffective.

This section is dedicated to three exceptional students whom I have taught. The first was a mature student, a prosecutor from Beijing. The second was also a mature student, a solicitor from Colombia. The third was a young student from South Korea. All three spoke English fairly well. All of them found that they had to translate from their native language into English as they spoke. While I was teaching them, I learned the technique described here. This technique applies to everyone, regardless of native language. My father taught me this rule: to learn a subject, teach it. Well, I am indebted to these students for teaching me how to get this point across.

Here is the technique:

- Start with the outline.
- Convert the outline into headlines.
- Keep your questions short.
- Keep your language simple.
- Keep your questions to a few before the next headline.

This is a formula for success for everybody, especially for lawyers grappling with language issues. Here is how it works.

The outline

START WITH THE outline. Language is not a barrier to thought. The student or lawyer can create an outline in any language and translate it into English in preparation time. The outline should contain subject or chapter headings (headlines) and the follow-up questions to make the point. The headlines introduce the subject and reduce the chance of confusion.

The headline

THE HEADLINE ALLOWS the witness to focus on what the examiner will discuss. This avoids the confusion that might arise where the language is less than clear.

Keep questions short

EACH QUESTION SHOULD be a few words. Perhaps ten or so words would be a good maximum. If a question cannot be kept short, the question can be rephrased or broken up into two or even three short questions. It should be a warning signal if the question is so complicated that it cannot be communicated in ten or so words.

Keep questions simple

NEXT, CHECK THE language, as the words should be simple. If there is a choice between two words, pick the simpler one. If English is not the first language of the examiner, there may be few ready choices. Nevertheless, consultation with a dictionary, thesaurus, or even a colleague should suffice. "Vehicle" becomes "car" or "truck," "incident" becomes "event," "numerous" becomes "many," and so on.

Finish the subject in a few questions

IF THE POINT to be made is shortened, the examiner can make it with a few questions. As a good practice, try to record the punchline in ten or so words. The punchline is the conclusion that the examiner wants the audience (the judge, usually) to draw from the headline and the few questions that follow. As an audit check, the headline should introduce the punchline, there should be a direct connection, and that connection should be the four or five questions between the beginning and the end. The questioner should not express the punchline out loud in court. It is the point to be made from the questions and answers in that short sequence.

The result of stringing together several headlines is the full direct examination or cross-examination. The creativity that goes into thinking up points is not one that is dependent upon language. The choice of words in the outline itself is a matter of technique, and with practice, this should cease to be an obstacle when posing the questions in real time — that is, during the examination itself.

EXAMPLE

CONSIDER THE FOLLOWING example. In the outline, the examiner (in chief) decides that the point to be made is that the driver approached the intersection with due attention to oncoming traffic.

HEADLINE. Now, I will ask you questions about when you came to the intersection.

Q. How fast were you driving?

Q. What lane were you in?

Q. Tell me about the traffic conditions?
Q. What were you paying attention to?
Q. What were your distractions?

HEADLINE. Now, I will ask you questions about the accident. . . .

The lawyer can take the answer to any of these questions and ask follow-up questions. Each of the questions could be a headline by itself, if the lawyer chooses to ask several questions about that subject. "How fast were you driving?" becomes "I will now ask about your speed."

A major benefit of asking short questions with simple language is that the judge will follow your line of questions. Each of the questions may appear in the notes of the judge as a word or two, possibly underlined, and each of the answers a couple of words right after that. With this simple question-and-answer system, the judge will get what the examiner and witness have to say — no matter what language is the examiner's first.

A word of caution. It is so easy to ask the next question right away after the answer that this can easily become a rapid-fire interrogation. Even in cross-examination, this should not be the objective. The judge will not be able to keep up, and the lawyer will start to trip over the words, whether simple or not.

Conclusion

SO LONG AS the session can be kept to short questions with simple language, the foreign language litigator can survive, even thrive. It will be creativity and technique that rule the day. Limited language skills will not serve as a constraint. This applies equally to novice lawyers. Their challenge may not be language, but rather the stress and distractions of trial work.

CASE STUDY

IN A SWIMMING pool accident, the lifeguard testifies (in chief) about how many kids used the pool that afternoon. Here is the sequence of questions from the outline:

Q. When did you come on duty to serve as lifeguard that afternoon?
Q. As lifeguard, what were the duties of your employment?
Q. How many kids were in the pool at midday, and how crowded was it?

Create a headline and short open questions to accomplish the same things.

Solution

HEADLINE. I will now ask about the pool that day.
Q. What was your job?
Q. When did you start that day?
Q. What were your duties?
Q. How many people were at the pool at midday?
Q. How crowded did that seem?

Interview Techniques

BEFORE LAWYERS INTERVIEW a witness in a case, they should prepare themselves to do so. This means that they should become familiar with whatever is known about the witness and what the witness has to offer. They should be aware of how the opposition sees the witness. Through case analysis, they should understand completely what they want to accomplish with the witness to succeed.

This brings us to the interview itself. Case analysis may provide an outline of what the witness is expected to say, but this does not mean that the lawyer should simply rely upon that case analysis for the entire outline for the interview. Indeed, what the lawyer does not know may turn out to be as important as what the lawyer does know.

Lawyers should be careful to let their own witnesses know why they will testify and what part of the story each will contribute — it should not be a state secret. Not all witnesses are allies in pursuit of a common goal. All witnesses who testify are inconvenienced to some extent. Most approach their testimony with some trepidation, and it is the role of the lawyer to ease the fears of the witnesses so that they perform at their best.

The interview should start with an explanation of the case from the perspective of the witness. A liability witness need not know about damages, and a breach of contract witness need not know about efforts to remedy the results of that breach. Nevertheless, witnesses should know the basic story to which they are asked to contribute. Following the explanation, lawyers should answer questions from the witness. Examples include the following:

- "When will I be called upon to testify?"
- "How long will that take?"

- "What arrangements do I have to make to get to and from the courthouse?"
- "Should I require a summons to witness?"
- "What happens if I don't show up?"
- "What happens if I make a mistake?"
- "What will I be asked?"
- "What will the other lawyer ask me?"

These are all good questions, and witnesses deserve respectful answers. With respect to the last two questions on the list, lawyers should be very careful to put witnesses through their paces. This may require that the lawyer conduct a direct examination as a practice round. It usually requires that the lawyer conduct a cross-examination.

If the lawyer dislikes what the witness has to say, the lawyer should reconsider calling the witness at all. If the witness will testify in any event, either by necessity or because of a subpoena issued by the other side, the lawyer should consider settling the case on less favourable terms.

During the interview, lawyers should be careful to ask the hard questions. Respect for the opposition warrants a thorough airing of what the witness has to offer. Even if it is not part of the case of the lawyer's client if it is part of the case of the opposition, the lawyer should be careful to put the point to the witness: "What will you say if you are asked this question?" The answer will inform how the lawyer treats the examination, and it may open avenues to how the lawyer deals with the elements of the case analysis. The hard questions will not go away simply because the lawyer chooses to ignore them.

Witnesses are people too

LAWYERS ARE VERY concerned about the perspectives of the parties. They should be equally concerned about the perspectives of their witnesses, which can be affected by many factors. Essentially, perspective can be broken down into three areas for consideration:

1. How is the witness today? Witnesses can be affected by poor memory, ill health, distractions in their own life, fear of cross-examination in this case, sympathy for one of the parties, and many other factors. Anything that can affect the quality of the testimony of the witness should be considered. Lawyers should be gentle but thorough in their interview to determine whether such factors will play a major influence.
2. How was the witness then? Just as the witness can be affected by current events and conditions, so the witness could have been affected by factors and conditions at the time of the events about which the witness will testify. Health, bias, distractions are all fair game for the interview. What was there about the witness and what was going on in the witness's life that can affect the quality of the testimony?
3. Lastly, there could be physical factors that influenced the ability of the witness to perceive the events. Remember that these physical factors may not be absolute. If there were two witnesses to an event, one may have been better situated to observe. Was one closer than the other, or was one better able to observe, because of obstacles, distractions, or other physical attributes in effect? How about eyesight and hearing

ability? Then there are absolute factors such as distance, climate conditions, speed of the occurrence of events, and the like that may play a role in either supporting or detracting from the credibility of the witness. Lawyers should be careful to include such questions in their interviews of witnesses.

Conclusion

IT MAY APPEAR obvious, but witnesses are an essential part of the presentation that the lawyer requires to succeed. Lawyers should treat their own witnesses as valuable assets.

The Art of Attentive Listening

"ATTENTIVE LISTENING" AND "active listening" are either synonymous or overlapping catchphrases commonly discussed of late. The central idea with respect to both is that the listener engage with the speaker.

Multi-tasking is a challenge faced by trial lawyers, indeed by everyone today. Lawyers worry about what is going on in the courtroom. They worry about their next question. They worry about what the judge or opposing counsel might think or do. There is so much going on! This complicates what is really a very simple transaction. The examiner asks, and then the witness answers. The examiner pauses to let the judge catch up. During the pause, the examiner frames the next question. Then repeat. What is so hard about that?

Attentive listening requires the listener to concentrate on the witness — that is all. The lawyer should forget other issues and just listen. Then the lawyer should let the next question reflect what the witness has said. Case analysis and the outline guide the lawyer, but it is the answer that is paramount.

If the witness did not respond to the question, the lawyer should reconsider the question. Perhaps it was poorly phrased. If so, the lawyer should try again. In cross-examination, the witness may try to dodge a hard question with an answer that does not address the question. If so, the lawyer should ask the question again. Whether the question was poorly phrased or the witness is being tactical, the examiner should pay close attention to what the witness has said.

Attentive listening theory includes body language and non-verbal feedback, none of which works well in court. Lawyers should stick to words. For example, this handbook discusses "looping" in Chapter 2, below, as a technique to assure the witness (and the audience) of the importance of certain answers. Another useful technique has the examiner make a general statement, followed by an open question in direct examination or a leading one in cross-examination.

EXAMPLE

THE WITNESS TESTIFIES that the weather seems to cause joint pain, consistent with arthritis. Consider these follow-up questions, one in direct examination and the other in cross-examination:

Q. [DIRECT] The weather that day was rainy and cold. How did that affect your arthritis?

Q. [CROSS] The weather that day was rainy and cold. That bothered you, correct?

In both cases, the witness's previous answer prompts the next question. The witness now has an opportunity to draw the connection between weather and arthritis on the day in question.

Conclusion

HOWEVER IT IS called, when lawyers pay attention to what the witnesses say, they are better placed to continue their examinations in a fruitful manner. This shows both respect and professionalism.

Relative Credibility — Is Mine Better Than Yours?

ONE MAJOR CHALLENGE that faces examiners in both direct examinations and cross-examinations is supporting the credibility of one witness and detracting from the credibility of another. The testimony of one is to be preferred to that of another. How is this done?

Lawyers often examine one witness in relation to another. In such cases, lawyers should keep in mind that there are many factors at play that would support or detract from the relative credibility of a witness. Consider the following factors:

- One witness has a better memory.
- One witness has professional or life experience in the area.

- One witness was distracted because of health, medication, alcohol, emotion, or personal involvement.
- One witness was closer to the scene, either in distance or in time.
- The observation of one witness was impaired by a visual (line of sight) or audio (competing noise) obstacle.
- One witness had experienced so many repetitions of the event that this one would not be memorable.
- One witness had more time to observe the event than did the other.
- One witness made notes of the event.
- One witness was trained and had experience in the observation of such events.

The English decision in *Browne v Dunn*[2] mandates that a cross-examiner confront the witness with the essence of any contradictory testimony that someone else will give later in the trial. This is a form of impeachment in that the witness's testimony contradicts something else to be presented to the court. The exercise could therefore follow the impeachment formula (to be presented in Chapter 5 of this handbook, below, which deals with cross-examinations). The first element of the formula is to confirm what the witness has to say. The second is to

2 (1893), 6 R 67 (HL). The rule in *Browne v Dunn* is summarized in *Allied Pastoral Holdings Pty Ltd v FCT* (1983), 1 NSWLR 1 at 16: "It is necessary to put to an opponent's witness in cross-examination the nature of the case upon which it is proposed to rely in contradiction of his evidence, especially where the case relies upon inferences to be drawn from other evidence in the proceedings."

establish what factors make the statement credible. The third is to identify how those factors apply to the other witness to support (in cross) or weaken (in direct) the reliability of that other source in relation to this witness.

When lawyers prepare to examine witnesses, their outlines should include questions that test relative credibility. They should raise these issues with the witness in the interview. The effort may suggest a form of inoculation and lead to better cross-examination of the other witnesses.

Conclusion

WHEN LAWYERS EXAMINE witnesses, they should always bear in mind that another witness may have something to say about the same subject. They should focus part of the examination on bolstering or detracting from what the other witness has to say.

CASE STUDY

IN A REAL estate transaction, the buyer consulted a lawyer. The lawyer will testify that the buyer knew about and accepted an easement at the back of the property. The buyer claims that this subject was never discussed in the meeting.

Create headlines and open questions to suggest that the buyer is more credible than the lawyer.

Solution

HEADLINE. I understand that the lawyer will say something different from what you say. Let's discuss that.

Q. How many times did you meet the lawyer?
A. Only once.
Q. How long did the meeting last?
A. Twenty minutes or so.
Q. What notes did the lawyer seem to make?
A. None when I was there.
Q. What notes did you make?
A. I kept notes on a pad. I have produced them to the court already.

HEADLINE. Let's talk about those notes.
Q. Why did you take notes?
A. Because the meeting was important to me.
Q. Why so?
A. Because this was a big deal to me.
Q. What do your notes say about the easement?
A. Nothing.
Q. Why not?
A. It was not discussed.
Q. The lawyer says otherwise. What do you say about that?
A. The lawyer is mistaken. If it was discussed, it would be in my notes.

chapter two

Techniques in Common for Examinations in General

EXAMINATIONS ARE, IN effect, controlled discussions. Two people speak with each other in the presence of an audience, the trial judge and opposing counsel (at least). The examiner leads the discussion in the sense that the questions direct what subjects the witness should address. There are several techniques common to both direct examinations and cross-examinations. It is common, for example, to follow up answers with more questions on the same subject or to use a word or phrase spoken by the witness or an idea expressed by the witness in a follow-up question (looping).

Examiners should control the momentum of the testimony (subtly in direct, not so subtly in cross). As with a movie director or orchestra conductor, the trial lawyer can create a favourable or unfavourable impression by the use of pace. Pauses, or the lack of them, are the most common method to manage the pace of the testimony of a witness. All examiners face the threat of objections. Nothing kills the momentum of an examination more effectively than a well-timed objection. A close rival for this as a momentum killer is an argument with the witness.

Lawyers who argue with their witnesses lose momentum, if not the point itself.

As with most of this handbook, the techniques suggested in this chapter are merely that, suggestions. When lawyers speak, they are the only ones responsible for what they say. This chapter will suggest several techniques that will help lawyers project professionalism and competence.

Follow-Up Questions

LAWYERS SHOULD BE able to follow up the answers given by witnesses with relevant questions. This applies to every situation in which lawyers ask questions, all the way from initial interviews with clients to interviews of witnesses to direct examinations and cross-examinations at trial. This subject features prominently in *The Art of the Interview*,[1] the first handbook published in this series. The follow-up technique requires the examiner to listen to the answer. This point should be obvious. Alas, it is ignored by many counsel — all wrapped up in their prepared questions, the only reason some lawyers listen to the answer is to know when it is polite to ask the next question on their list.

The ability to follow up is a discrete skill: it requires practice. Consider any fact or point, any one. Then run off a series of follow-up questions, all open questions, at least for the purpose of this drill.

---

1 John Hollander, *The Art of the Interview: How Lawyers Talk With Clients* (Toronto: Irwin Law, 2013), online: www.irwinlaw.com/titles/art-interview.

EXAMPLE

THE FACT UNDER discussion is that the pen had black ink. Follow-up questions include the following:

- "What pen are we talking about?"
- "Whose pen was it?"
- "Where was it?"
- "Describe the pen."
- "What was the brand of the pen?"
- "What colour was the ink?"
- "Where did the pen come from?"
- "Who knew about the pen?"
- "What notes did you make about the pen?"
- "What literature described the pen?"

It is obvious that many of these questions are trivial and even silly, but the purpose of the demonstration is to show how many questions can follow up a simple statement of fact. Witnesses answer open questions in direct examination with answers that beg for more detail. With practice, lawyers can become expert at following a trail wherever it leads.

Note that the follow-up questions identify single facts. Where the first question in a series may have been an open question that allowed for multiple facts in the response, the follow-ups seek a single fact each. This allows the examiner to zero in on exactly the point to be made.

This is not only a technique for direct examinations. In cross-examinations, witnesses often give longer answers, and answers may also be non-responsive or unexpected. Lawyers can seize the opportunity to ask short, pointed, and leading questions to follow this lead. This creates opportunity. The lawyer's goal should be to accomplish something on the agenda: help the case, harm the case of the opponent, boost or attack credibility. This is just as true in cross-examinations as it is in direct examinations.

Conclusion

FOLLOW-UP QUESTIONS PERMIT lawyers to explore a subject fully with single facts. This allows the judge the chance to appreciate the significance of the evidence. Without listening, examiners risk the failure to exploit opportunities as they arise.

CASE STUDY

IN A CUSTODY case, the examiner is conducting the direct examination of the non-custodial parent. The parent gives this answer to an open question:

A. I went to pick up my child at four o'clock from daycare.

List ten follow-up open questions that might arise from this answer. Ignore the possibility that some are not germane to the issue or that they may repeat questions that might have preceded this answer.

Solution

Q. Where was the daycare?
Q. How long had your child been there that day?
Q. How long did it take you to get there?
Q. Please show me the daycare contract.

Q. How much did daycare cost?
Q. By what route did you get there that day?
Q. How did you usually get there?
Q. When did you usually arrive?
Q. By what means of transportation did you usually get there?
Q. What means did you use that day?
Q. Who saw you pick up your child that day?
Q. Who was in charge of the daycare that day?
Q. What did you say to the person in charge, if anything?
Q. What records are there to confirm the time of the pickup?

Punchlines

PUNCHLINES ARE SHORT phrases that make a point. They are commonly used in advertising. In court, they are the summary conclusion of what the examiner wants the audience to conclude, but they are not evidence in and of themselves. Unlike advertising punchlines, they may not even be spoken out loud.

There is a major difference between punchlines in direct examinations and in cross-examinations. In direct, the witness delivers the line, like the funny member of a comedy team. In cross, however, the punchline can be either spoken or implied. If spoken aloud, the lawyer uses the punchline in the form of a leading question, to which the witness indicates agreement (one hopes):

Q. So you were in a hurry, is that correct?

If unspoken, it is the inevitable conclusion of a series of answers. In this case, no one actually speaks the punchline. For the lawyer to put the punchline to the witness as a final question in the sequence invites the witness to retract or explain. This becomes the dreaded "question too many." The technique of the unspoken punchline is explored in greater length in Chapter 5, below.

The purpose of each sequence of five-and-out in both direct examination and cross-examination is to make a single point. In preparing the outline, the examiner should express that point as a punchline. This allows the examiner to determine whether the point was accomplished during the actual examination in court. If so, the advocate can rely upon that point later in examinations and in submissions.

The lawyer should have prepared an outline for the witness's examination. During preparation, case analysis directed what points should be established through the witness. Before the examination, counsel should consider how the testimony will sound. A pattern of headline, followed by five questions, followed by punchline (spoken or implied) creates a steady stream or rhythm. The benefits of this technique are the following:

- It helps the lawyer stay on message.
- It helps build the confidence of the witness in direct, and destroy the confidence of the witness in cross.
- It allows the judge to follow the logic of the testimony.
- It may give the impression to the witness and to opposing counsel that the lawyer is accomplish-

ing more than is in fact the case. This has its own merits.

This process permits the lawyer to act as a movie director without the witness appearing to read from a script. It is a fine line indeed between a witness who is prepared and one who is coached. Like good art, it is in the eyes of the beholder, in this case the trial judge. Unlike art, it is also governed by professional conduct rules. Witnesses are better able to use the language of a punchline if prompted by a headline and a few targeted questions. In cross, the same applies to a judge, who can draw the inference based upon a few short questions all of which lead to "yes" replies.

EXAMPLES

Direct examination

IT IS EASY for the witness to follow the sequence to a suitable punchline:

HEADLINE. Let's talk about the barn.
Q. Where was it?
A. In the northeast corner of the Jones farm.
Q. What was it made of?
A. It was built from wood and then painted.
Q. What colour?
A. Blue.
Q. And how did that stand out?
A. It was the only bright-blue barn in the whole county.

The punchline in this case is not only that the barn was blue but that it was remarkable and stood out. It is spoken by the witness, not by the direct examiner.

Cross-examination

HEADLINE. I'm going to ask you some questions about the barn.

Q. It was on the Jones farm, correct?

A. Yes.

Q. In the northeast corner, correct?

A. Yes.

Q. It was made of wood, correct?

A. Yes.

Q. It was painted blue, correct?

A. Yes.

Q. And it was the only blue barn in the county, correct?

A. Yes.

Although the witness did not speak it as a punchline, the conclusion is identical to the point made in the direct examination sequence. The cross-examiner did not ask, "So the barn must have stood out, correct?" Nevertheless, that is the conclusion (or punchline) from the sequence.

Conclusion

THE PUNCHLINE ALSO serves as a bridge from one sequence of questions to the next. The examiner leaves the point to move on to the next headline. The examiner may use an exaggerated pause to let the point sink in, which allows the judge to record the conclusion that the cross-examiner or the witness has just made.

Looping

THIS TECHNIQUE USES the word or phrase of the witness in the next question. It can be very annoying when the technique is used too often. However, it can also be very effective. Looping avoids the rule against examiners' putting words into the mouths of their witnesses. Once the witness uses the word (such as hurry, sloppy, lazy), it becomes fair game for the examiner to use. Looping also allows the examiner to emphasize something that is important and that has just been said by the witness — it is a way to underline the concept. The word or phrase may be significant to the witness, to the examiner, or to both.

Where the witness thinks that the word is significant, the lawyer's follow-up should explore the reason for its significance. Perhaps the witness observed a feature of the person or object in question. The lawyer's follow-up uses the word but asks why it is significant to the witness.

EXAMPLE

Q. What did you notice about the other driver?
A. Her hands were shaking like a leaf in the wind.
Q. Why were her shaking hands important to you?
A. Because they showed how nervous she was.

The witness may not think that the word is significant, but the examiner does. In this case, the examiner follows up with questions that use the word in sequence.

EXAMPLE

Q. Tell me about how the board made its decision.
A. It was made in haste, in my opinion.
Q. How hasty was it?
A. It was over in, like, three minutes.
Q. How important was this hasty decision to the other directors?
A. It risked the whole enterprise.

Witnesses sometimes use emotionally loaded words. Lawyers should tread carefully when trying to introduce such words, but when the witness introduces them, they are free for use.

EXAMPLE

Q. What did you make of that communication?
A. Well, that was a betrayal of my trust.

Looping follow-ups:

Q1. What was the betrayal?
Q2. How did that betray your trust?
Q3. How did that betrayal affect you?

The word "betrayal" is loaded with emotion. Lawyers generally cannot use this kind of evocative language in a question without facing a strenuous objection, which may well be sustained. However, once the witness has used the word, the lawyer is free to ask the follow-ups as set out above. The technique applies equally in direct examinations and cross-examinations.

EXAMPLE

CONSIDER THIS SEQUENCE in the direct examination of the wife and mother in a custody case:

Q. Why did you not visit your children on the weekend?
A. Because my husband was angry and abusive to me in the phone call on the Thursday.

Looping follow-ups:

Q1. How angry did he appear?
Q2. What abusive things did he say?
Q3. How often was he angry and abusive to you?
Q4. Where else did he direct his anger and abuse?

Conclusion

LOOPING IS A technique that allows the examiner to capitalize on the language used by the witness. It can introduce or reinforce a concept to advance the examiner's agenda.

CASE STUDY

IN A WRONGFUL dismissal lawsuit, the employee takes the position that the behaviour of the employer was heavy-handed and warrants aggravated damages.

1. During the direct examination of the employee, the employee answers a question this way: "After calling me into the management office, my boss ripped me to shreds. I was completely humiliated." Prepare two questions that follow up the statements using the looping technique.

2. During cross-examination, the same employee testifies, "Of course, the meeting was held in secrecy. No one was able to witness what happened." Prepare two leading questions that follow up the statements using the looping technique.

Solution

Direct examination

Q1. How did your boss rip you to shreds?

Q2. What humiliating words did your boss use?

Cross-examination

Q1. Secrecy worked in your favour, didn't it?

Q2. If no one was there to see it, the humiliation was reduced, was it not?

The Value of the Pause

LITIGATORS HAVE TO be public speakers. Oddly, many hate to speak in public, with the audience in front of them; but put the spectators behind them and give them a witness, and they shine. The point is that trials require that lawyers learn and master some of the techniques of rhetoric. Cadence, voice pitch and volume, and use of the pause are examples of these techniques. The one most easily mastered and most appreciated by judges and witnesses alike, is the pause.

Many lawyers speak too quickly, and when they do, witnesses cannot follow the question, and judges cannot make effective notes of the testimony. The solution is to pause. Junior lawyers should make a reminder note in their outlines to pause after the witness answers. They should listen to the answer. They might glance at the judge, and if the judge is still writing, the lawyer should wait patiently. When the judge catches up, a nod from the judge will prompt the next question. This is extra true for punchlines. The pause allows the judge to draw and record the conclusion that the lawyer has just made.

Unfortunately, lawyers often do not listen well. Pauses encourage the lawyer to listen, if only because nothing happens during the pause. The lawyer may well consider the previous answer: Where should it lead? The best next question may not be the one recorded in the lawyer's outline.

Now consider this from the perspective of the audience, which may be the trial judge, but this applies equally to audiences of all kinds. The testimony is supposed to inform the audience, after all, not just feed a transcript. Pausing encourages the lawyer to adapt the delivery to fit the ability of the judge to keep up. This requires the judge to hear, process, and record the evidence. Without pauses, judges may have difficulty drawing the conclusions that the examiner wants, and this defeats the purpose of the examination. Few judges can hear, process, and record information as quickly as lawyers can put questions to the witness. Lawyers should give judges a break. They should moderate the pace to let judges do their work.

Here are the advantages of building a pause into the rhythm of question, answer, question, answer:

- It offsets quick speech. No matter how hard junior lawyers try, they will still speak too quickly.
- It allows the witness to follow the question. This avoids confusion, interruptions, and distractions.

- It helps develop rapport between the examiner and the judge.
- It creates the space necessary for the judge to appreciate and record the points as they are made.

WARNING

IN BOTH DIRECT examinations and cross-examinations, witnesses tend to fill the dead air created when lawyers pause. Lawyers should prepare their witnesses to avoid this, in direct examinations. In the case of cross-examinations, lawyers who prepare witnesses should caution them as well. Witnesses often do not know what is going on around them — testifying can be a harrowing experience, after all. They may think that the silence is bad. They may feel that the silence is their fault, somehow, and conclude that the remedy is to speak. Lawyers should make the witnesses understand that the pause is an opportunity to reflect, not a licence to improvise.

Conclusion

BY USING THE simple rhetorical device of pausing after an answer, the junior lawyer can accomplish a great deal. Of all the rhetorical techniques, this is the easiest one to practise and learn. It can be practised before a mirror, with the record function of a cell phone, or it can be observed by colleagues and more senior lawyers.

Hurry Slowly

TRIAL LAWYERS ARE told, "Be quick, but be thorough." This is quite a dilemma. The same challenge faces every examiner with respect to each witness: how to wrap up the witness's testimony quickly yet allow the judge to listen, appreciate, and record it all. This section presents some techniques to resolve that dilemma.

Listen carefully

THE FIRST TECHNIQUE is not actually a tactic. Most lawyers speak too quickly, and without acting lessons, lawyers cannot change their speech habits. It is a major distraction for young lawyers. Instead, they should concentrate on the answer of the witness and then on the next question. If they try to moderate their behaviour while thinking of the next question, they may overload their real-time abilities.

Pause after each answer

THE SECOND TECHNIQUE may be the best and easiest of all. As discussed in "The Value of the Pause," above, lawyers should pause after each answer. They should pause even longer after each sequence of questions. Unless the goal is to unnerve the witness in cross-examination, lawyers should avoid the rapid-fire question style, as such behaviour will lose the sympathy of the judge and should be used only rarely.

Think of the next question before you ask it

THE NEXT TECHNIQUE requires the lawyer to consider the next question during the pause following the previous answer. The right question asked after some thought is far better than a poor question asked in haste. Young lawyers fear the silence of dead air while they consider their next question. But actually, this pause is appreciated. The witness usually wants a break, however brief, and the trial judge can think about the testimony and will sympathize with the lawyer who tries to get it right.

Headlines

THIS TECHNIQUE APPEARS to slow the process, but it does not work that way. Headlines promote efficient use of time. Much time is wasted if the witness is confused by a question.

One fact at a time

THE NEXT TECHNIQUE consists of limiting each question to a single fact. In direct examination, this may not be possible or practical when the lawyer introduces the subject, because the witness should give a full answer, and this may involve several facts. Direct examiners can follow up with questions that isolate individual facts. Start broadly, then follow up specifically. For example, consider the headline "I will now ask questions about the meeting that took place at head office." The first question may well be, "Please tell me what happened at that meeting." Clearly, this does not lend itself to a single-fact answer. But by asking follow-up questions restricted to single facts, the examiner can accomplish the same result.

Simple language

THE NEXT TECHNIQUE obliges lawyers to use simple language. Lawyers know what they are asking, but do the witnesses? Witnesses are confused by the use of long or technical words, or complicated phrase structures. In preparing the outline, the examiner (both direct and cross) should consider how to pose the question. If it may require language that is difficult to digest, the examiner can break it into two or more questions. Replacing difficult words or phrases with simple ones may take effort, but it is far better that this effort take place during preparation than during the examination in real time.

"Please explain"

THE NEXT TECHNIQUE consists of two simple words, "please explain." Where the answer to a question may be difficult to understand, the lawyer should ask the witness to explain. The judge may chime in with "That's okay, counsellor. I get it." If so, the lawyer can move on, but if not, the lawyer should give the judge the benefit of an explanation. This way, the lawyer can be sure that the questions elicited the points that the lawyer wanted to establish. If they did not, the lawyer can ask suitable questions to make those points.

Avoid "and" and "or"

THE NEXT TECHNIQUE requires that the lawyer avoid conjunctions and other words that combine two or more thoughts. Examples include "but," "without," "unless," "and," "or," etc. These combinations may be difficult for the witness and the judge to follow. It is not always possible to avoid conjunctions, but it is frequently helpful when it can be accomplished. Often, the conjunction adds a second fact. This may confuse the witness (in direct) or allow the witness to argue or evade (in cross). Both of these results are distracting.

Conclusion

A WELL-PLANNED, WELL-IMPLEMENTED examination (direct or cross) will impress the trial judge and opposing counsel. This will reward the lawyer and reduce trial time — mission accomplished.

Objections

THE RULES OF evidence are intertwined with the rules of civil procedure. Witnesses testify, but they may only testify with admissible evidence. Evidence can be admitted through testimony (orally, by affidavit or transcript) or by exhibit. In the case of oral evidence, there are restrictions. How does a lawyer ask a specific question? What answer is the witness called upon to give? These are two of the major points that bring about objections. This is not a handbook about the rules of evidence. It is, however, a handbook about trial practice, and the principles regarding objections are governed by the latter.

Object rarely

THE FIRST PRINCIPLE is to object as little as possible. Objections presume that the examiner has strayed from the accepted path, and repeated objections will cause some stress in the relationship between counsel. They also interrupt the flow of the evidence, they distract the trial judge, and they may cause the witness some confusion. Should the witness answer? Should the witness pause? What is going on? So the first rule is object rarely.

Pick your spots

LAWYERS SHOULD RAISE objections only when it matters. The nature of the question or the answer should be of significance, which is, of course, a judgment call by counsel. Nevertheless, lawyers should be able to express not only the legal basis of the objection but also, at least in private, the material impact of the point (whether question or answer) that led to the objection in the first place. It should be kept in mind that the trial judge may raise objections as well. If it does not bother the trial judge, perhaps it should not bother counsel. So the second rule is object when it is important.

Be right

THE COROLLARY OF the second rule is that judges and counsel have little patience with needless interruption. Therefore lawyers who object had better be right when they do. If they face repeated "overruled" decisions, they will have caused harm to their own cause. So the third rule is make each shot count.

Be civil

A GOVERNING PRINCIPLE is to object politely — firmly but politely. The objection is not directed to the examiner but rather to the trial judge. During the course of the objection, there may be submissions by one or by both lawyers. All submissions are directed to the trial judge and not to the opposing lawyer. So the fourth rule is object civilly.

The formula

OBJECTIONS FOLLOW AN accepted ritual. In theory, there are four stages to the objection. First is the warning, communicated with the words "I object" or, simply, "objection." Second is the legal basis for the objection, whether it calls for opinion, hearsay, speculation, or another ground. Third is the submission phase, where lawyers argue the merits of the objection (if called upon to do so). The final phase is the ruling. Here it is, broken down with greater detail:

1. The lawyer who objects must always rise. When the objecting lawyer stands, the examiner should sit. Only one lawyer should stand at a time. Standing calls for attention, and the trial judge can address only one person at a time. To get the judge's attention, the objecting lawyer states, "I object." That starts the ritual.
2. The lawyer states the basis for the objection concisely. One sentence or phrase of a few words will suffice. Examples include the following:
   - "That question calls for speculation."
   - "That question calls for hearsay."
   - "Counsel is leading the witness."
   - "Asked and answered."
3. After the lawyer states the objection, the trial judge has full control of the process. The judge may ask the objecting lawyer to state the grounds, and this

becomes a submission. Or the judge may ask the examiner to explain why the question should be permitted. If so, the objecting lawyer sits, and the examiner stands and then makes submissions.

4. After the judge has received enough information upon which to make a decision, the judge will make a ruling. If the ruling sustains the objection, the question may not be asked; however, if the judge overrules the objection, the question must be answered.
5. In all cases, both lawyers should say, "Thank you, Your Honour," as if to say, "No hard feelings."

It is acceptable for the examiner to short-circuit this affair by simply rephrasing the question or abandoning the subject and moving on to another one.

Tactical objections

LAWYERS MAY USE objections for the sole purpose of disrupting the flow of the question and answer from opposing counsel. These are called tactical objections, and they are . . . , well, objectionable. Perhaps the lawyer does not like the way that the questions are being asked or answered. Perhaps the lawyer wants to somehow protect the witness. Even worse, sometimes the lawyer wants to deliver a signal to the witness, such as to suggest an answer. Whatever the motivation, tactical objections are unethical and improper, and litigators should never use objections for this purpose.

Timing

THE TIMING OF objections is important. Objections that are raised after the evidence has been received can be compared to closing the barn door after the livestock have escaped. Even though trial judges are sophisticated enough to disregard objectionable testimony, it is far better to attack the question before the answer is given.

Often, the question calls for an admissible answer. The witness, however, does not know what is and is not admissible and may answer with inadmissible testimony, such as an opinion or hearsay. In that case, it is not the question to which opposing counsel objects but rather the answer, and it is appropriate for the objecting lawyer to raise the objection during the witness's answer.

Common objections

WITH THIS IN mind, here are the most common objections made in the evidence phase at trial:

- "Objection, that calls for speculation." For example, the examiner asked the witness to identify why another person said something. Who can know what goes through the mind of another person? If the witness knows the answer only because the other person explained the reason, the objection may well involve hearsay.
- "Objection, that calls for an opinion for which this witness has not been qualified." Even qualified experts are restricted from giving opinions outside their area of qualified expertise. Keep in mind that

lay witnesses may give opinions in some circumstances.

- "Objection, that calls for hearsay." For example, the examiner asked the witness to recite what another witness said. The exceptions to the hearsay rule are legion, and whether one of the exceptions applies becomes a matter for submissions.
- "Objection, that question assumes facts not in evidence." For example, the question presumed that the door to the kitchen was closed, and there was no evidence that this door was closed or open. Is it premature to put the question to the witness in that fashion?
- "Objection, counsel is leading the witness." If the matter is controversial, the lawyer should not put questions to the witness to which the answer is repeatedly suggested.
- "Objection, that question has been asked and answered."
- "Objection, the question is vague/irrelevant/misleading/ambiguous." The record will not clearly connect the answer to the question. If the question is overly vague or ambiguous, the witness cannot know what question to answer. Often, lawyers cram two questions into a single effort. Which should the witness try to answer?

Conclusion

THIS HAS BEEN a simple primer on how and when to object during the evidence phase of a civil trial. The basic principles are to object rarely but, if necessary, to object effectively. Anything else will distract and annoy the trial judge, and more harm than good comes from this.

CASE STUDY

IN A NUISANCE case, oil leaked from a tank on AB's land and polluted CD's land. AB is testifying in chief.

State the objection to each of these questions:

Q1. What happened when CD saw the leak and called you out on it?
Q2. Why did CD call you?
Q3. What did the installer tell you about the life of the oil tank?
Q4. The cleanup crew came right away, right?

Solution

O1. I object. The question is vague and compound. It seems to ask for answers to two or more questions.
O2. I object. The question calls for speculation.
O3. I object. The question calls for hearsay.
O4. I object. Counsel is leading on a sensitive matter.

Using the Clock During Examinations

THE CLOCK IS a fact of life in litigation, and lawyers ignore this at their peril. This section discusses some of the timing issues that trial lawyers face.

It is common knowledge that people have a limited ability to concentrate and absorb information. They can listen attentively for between thirty and sixty minutes, depending upon the person and the subject matter.

Clearly, some presentations are more entertaining than others. People tend to be fresher in the morning than in the afternoon.

Note that this is equally true for witnesses. A witness who has waited in the hall for hours will be in poor shape to testify and will require a more gentle approach. A longer introduction will assist the witness to acclimate to the courtroom.

The court clock seems to operate in increments (sessions) of approximately seventy-five to ninety minutes. Judges take breaks at midmorning, lunch hour, and midafternoon. This means that as much as one-third of the testimony of a daylong witness may occur when the judge — who is just as human as the witnesses — cannot pay close attention.

Here are some tips for using the clock:

- Try to make the most important points early in a session.
- For matters that are difficult to grasp, make sure that the break does not interrupt the presentation. If it does, be prepared to conduct a recap as the next session begins.
- Save the weakest part of the testimony for later in the session.
- If asked to start an examination toward the end of a session, start with the weakest material.
- As the session wears on, use headlines with increasing frequency.
- As the session wears on, be prepared to highlight, underline, accent, or repeat important information

as it comes out. The looping technique may work well here.

- Look for an appropriate time for a break, and then suggest that the judge call a recess at that time. Time the more dramatic information for immediately following the break.
- Ask for a recess as the longer examination (direct or cross) winds down. This permits the examiner to check notes or consult a colleague, expert, or client. In the case of cross-examination, it also permits the creation of a thoughtful final five-and-out sequence based on what has occurred to that point to wind up on a high note.
- In cross-examination, witnesses tire more easily than counsel, and they put up less effective defences as the session wears on. Consider when to make some of the points, as fatigue also makes witnesses testy, more argumentative.
- Headline — short questions — simple language: This formula becomes more significant as the attention of the judge starts to wander.

If this sounds like choreography of a stage play, there is some reason for that. Dramatists know how to capture the imagination of their audience, and as a litigator, there is some requirement for exactly this skill.

Conclusion

THERE CAN BE a downside to using the clock: it can be distracting to the examiner. Junior litigators have enough to worry about without pretending to be theatre directors. Put the substance before the appearance. Nevertheless, when to ask for a recess and when to delay asking certain questions will be judgment calls for counsel to make. This is using the clock.

Arguing With a Witness

HERE IS THE best advice that a junior litigator considering when to argue with the witness will hear: Don't, ever. Litigators often hear what they consider to be silly, spiteful, petty, and downright objectionable testimony, which appears to beg for argument. Litigators should resist the urge. Mark Twain once wrote, "A gentleman is someone who knows how to play the banjo and doesn't." Paraphrased, a litigator is someone who knows how to argue and doesn't, at least with witnesses.

What is arguing with the witness? Simply put, argument is a series of statements made to the witness that are not questions. If the witness does not have an opportunity to respond to each statement, as a question, this is argument. If the witness cannot get a word in edgewise, this is argument.

Where a witness says something that calls for argument, how is the lawyer to react? The best response is to ask a series of questions that makes the statement from the witness appear to be as silly, spiteful, petty, and objectionable as the cross-examiner deems it to be. When the witness is on the stand, the examiner's best weapon is the next question. When the witness has finished testifying, the lawyer can argue as much as is appropriate.

Just because the examiner finds the testimony to be objectionable, this does not mean that the trial judge considers it to be so. The lawyer has the "power of the pulpit," and by arguing with the witness, the lawyer abuses this power. The argument will prompt a response from the bench or counsel table: "Objection! Will counsel please stop badgering the witness?"

There are three basic problems with argument:

1. The trial judge may not be able to follow it. Arguments tend to consist of rapid-fire statements made by both counsel and witness — too quick for a judge to follow.
2. It is not testimony. There is nothing factual for the trial judge to glean that will assist the understanding of the case.
3. There is an apparent imbalance of power between witness and lawyer. The lawyer stands and gets to move around. The lawyer gets to shape the questions and language used. The sympathy of the audience may well rest with the witness, regardless of what prompted the argument in the first place. Basically, the lawyer cannot win the argument.

Conclusion

THE LAWYER'S WEAPON during the examination is the question. The major advantage that the lawyer has over the witness is the lawyer gets to win the point in closing argument, with the witness off the witness stand and unable to respond.

CASE STUDY

THE HOMEOWNER HIRES a contractor to repair the kitchen cabinets. The $5,000 contract becomes a $20,000 dispute about extra work and overcharging. In cross-examination, the contractor points a finger at the examiner's client and says, "Well, that twit [the owner] told me to keep working without ever asking for my opinion."

Create a headline and a few leading questions to make this appear to be the contractor's fault.

Solution

HEADLINE. Let's discuss what your role was.

Q. The owner hired you, correct?

A. Yes.

Q. To repair the kitchen cabinets, correct?

A. Yes.

Q. You said you could do the job, correct?

A. Yes.

Q. And do it well, correct?

A. Yes.

Q. The twit took you at your word, correct?

A. Yes.

PUNCHLINE. [UNSPOKEN] That makes you responsible for what happened.

When Questions Are Distasteful in Cross-examination

SOME QUESTIONS CAN be distasteful to the cross-examiner, to the witness, to the trial judge, or to any combination of the three. What should the cross-examiner do in that case? There are really only two choices. The cross-examiner should either avoid the subject altogether or raise the subject in as inoffensive a manner as possible. There are certain subjects that must be raised during cross-examination, and these are not only the hard questions. These can be questions that involve very sensitive subjects. There are culturally sensitive subjects that people have been taught to avoid. These subjects may be different among different demographics or cultural groups, but they nevertheless exist.

Occasionally, there is a third option available to counsel. The lawyer can hand the cross-examination over to another lawyer who does not face the same reluctance. Perhaps it is best if counsel of a different age, gender, race, or religion conduct the cross? This is one of the advantages to working in teams.

Lawyers should be alert to the sensitivities of their audience, both the witness and the judge, but they should be less sensitive to what drives them. If the subject is one that the lawyer considers to be personally distasteful, the lawyer should get over it. Either the question is important or it is not. If it is important, the job requires that it be canvassed. Case analysis and professional competence standards make this obligatory. Remember the admonition about heat and kitchens.

The witness or trial judge may find a subject to be offensive. In that case, the lawyer should approach the subject with greater tact. The lawyer may be incorrect in assuming that the witness or judge will find the subject offensive. The lawyer can alert the judge to the possibility and seek directions, and with leave, the question can take place in camera, away from the prying eyes of the public and the witness.

In direct examination, the lawyer can change the type of questions from open to leading with the permission of the court. In cross-examination, the lawyer can dial down the level of aggression used in the questioning method, and, indeed, the lawyer can even switch to using gentle open questions if the result does not pose unnecessary risk. The purpose of this change in method is to allow the witness to discuss the subject without the appearance of bullying. If the lawyer shows delicacy, this will encourage the witness to discuss the subject as openly as possible.

Conclusion

WHAT IS SENSITIVE is a matter of judgment. How the lawyer deals with the sensitive subject is itself another matter calling for the exercise of judgment. As lawyers become more experienced, this becomes less problematic.

CASE STUDY

IN A PERSONAL injury claim, the plaintiff alleges that the injury impaired the sex life of the plaintiff and spouse. In chief, counsel wants to establish that both the frequency and the quality of sexual relations have declined. In cross, counsel wants to attack this — gently. Fortunately, counsel asked about this in discovery, so the subject has been dealt with in advance.

Create the headlines and questions to deal with this sensitive subject.

Solution

Direct examination

HEADLINE. Let's now deal with the subject of your relations with your spouse.

Q. How has this injury affected your sex life?

Q. Tell us about how it was before the accident?

Q. How important is this change to you?

Q. Please tell us more about that.

Cross-examination

HEADLINE. I am afraid I have to ask some sensitive questions about how this accident has affected your sex life.

Q. You did not keep track of the times you had sex with your spouse, did you?

Q. And you did not record how you felt about it, did you?

Q. And neither did your spouse, is that correct?

Q. And you did not tell others about your relations, did you?

Q. You did not tell your doctor either, did you?

PUNCHLINE. [UNSPOKEN] We have only your word for it.

chapter three

The Trial Judge

THIS IS A handbook about courtroom examinations, and as such, it must deal with one of the essential participants — the trial judge. This handbook discusses several issues that confront the trial lawyer, many of which are simple, commonsense. However, advocates often do not consider how the judge perceives the drama unfolding in the courtroom. One of the essential themes of all the handbooks in this series is that the lawyer must consider the other people in the room. Seen from the perspective of these other participants, the case is entirely different.

For a trial lawyer conducting an examination, there are always two other people who are critically important to success: the witness and the trial judge. In most cases, there is also a third person who matters, opposing counsel. And often, there are other people who matter, such as clients and opposing parties. This chapter deals with the plight of the overworked, underappreciated trial judge.

Consider the mandate of the judge. Really, there are three:

- Do justice to the case being heard.
- Protect the witness and maintain order in the court.
- Finish the case to make room for the next one.

By tradition and common practice, the trial judge has a different vantage point, at the front of the courtroom. Often the judge sits elevated above the trial lawyers, witnesses, and other participants. In arbitrations, the courtroom may be laid out differently, but the idea is the same — the decision maker has to sit apart from the other participants.

Consider these questions:

- How does the trial lawyer ensure that the judge actually understands and appreciates the significance of the points being made?
- What should the trial lawyer do if the judge does not appear to have received the information transmitted?
- What should the trial lawyer do if the judge prevents with interruptions and interventions the transmission of that information?

All of these questions are dealt with in this chapter.

The Judge's Pen

LAWYERS ARE TAUGHT from an early stage that "delivery" means both transmission and reception. The two-way nature of communication requires that the judge receive the information the lawyer is seeking to transmit. This means that the lawyer has to accommodate the trial judge in various ways. How can the trial lawyer help the judge absorb and appreciate the evidence? This is the subject of *The Civil Courtroom*,[1] another handbook in this series. This section will focus on the judge's pen — yes, the pen.

While judges try to watch the witness and the examining lawyer, it is all that they can handle to make notes of what they observe, and they also try to make notes of what they think about and what they hear. With a steady increase in their workload, how can judges recall the evidence — and their take on it — when they reserve decisions until later?

To be most effective, trial lawyers should adapt their activities to the pace at which the judge can absorb the information adduced, which requires the judge to listen, appreciate, and record. For obvious reasons, listening takes the same time as speaking. While the lawyer is considering the next question, the judge records what was just said. Then add time for the judge to process the testimony, to appreciate its significance:

- Does it make sense?
- What does it mean?
- Is it credible?
- How does it compare to other evidence?
- How do people normally act?
- What is the legal significance?

All of these questions should be front and centre in a trial lawyer's mind. After all, if the judge fails to grasp what the lawyer has accomplished, then the lawyer has failed. The easiest way that the lawyer can help the judge

1 John Hollander, *The Civil Courtroom: Professionalism to Build Rapport* (Toronto: Irwin Law, 2013), online: www.irwinlaw.com/titles/civil-courtroom.

is to watch the pen — no, not while the lawyer is speaking. Multi-tasking is not all that it is cracked up to be. Ask the witness a question. Listen to the answer. Pause after the answer to the question is given. Consider the next question. This allows the judge the opportunity to consider the answer just given. The judge's pen will tell you when enough time has passed.

If the judge keeps writing, maybe the lawyer has asked two questions in one, maybe the witness has given too much information. Five-and-outs (discussed in Chapter 1, above) allow the lawyer to break the testimony into bite-sized chunks, which should be easily digested. However, evidence does not always emerge according to plan, and some witnesses give long answers, complex answers, technical answers, or unexpected answers. If lawyers listen carefully and watch the judge's pen, they can ask their witnesses to explain, to break their long answers into shorter ones, or to translate their technical answers into lay language.

Conclusion

THE JUDGE'S PEN will tell the trial lawyer a great deal. The lawyer should welcome all hints about what the judge thinks, and the pen provides some of those hints. Add to that the value of the judge's gratitude for easing the load. This is a great technique for young counsel to get ahead.

Interruptions by the Trial Judge

INTERRUPTIONS ARE USUALLY considered impolite, but at trial, there is a major exception — when the trial judge interrupts. Anything said by the trial judge during the course of the trial represents information, valuable information: What is the judge thinking? What annoys the judge? How patient is the judge with this evidence? How else should the evidence be presented? How well or badly is the case going?

When judges interrupt, lawyers should consider carefully what is being communicated. Consider these possibilities:

- Perhaps the lawyer's question may have been inappropriate (such as calling for inadmissible evidence). If so, the lawyer should rephrase.
- Perhaps the judge wants some other question answered by the witness. In that case, the lawyer should consider how to bring that evidence forward. Is the current witness the best way to accomplish this?
- If the judge is informing the lawyer of some impropriety, the lawyer should consider how to change the way the lawyer is going about things.
- If the judge is acting impatient, maybe it is time to suggest a recess. The judge may not be appreciating the evidence presented.

Each of these examples represents valuable information received from the trial judge.

Occasionally, the trial judge will direct a question to the witness. The direct examiner can warn the witness in advance that this may happen. The witness should then direct the response to the judge, and not to the examiner. Where the lawyer was going to ask the question anyway, it is acceptable for the lawyer to tell the judge politely that the question is coming up and that the judge should be patient. The judge may want to hear the answer right away, in which case the lawyer should obey the direction.

What is awkward is when the judge asks a question that is itself objectionable. Perhaps the question was poorly phrased, or the question calls for inadmissible evidence. If so, the lawyer should object. Even though the trial judge is responsible for the question, the lawyer should take a principled position with respect to the evidence. This may be decisive in an appeal.

Junior litigators usually defer to the trial judge, and correctly so. Nevertheless, lawyers should remember that they are responsible to their clients for the proper presentation of the case. If this means standing up to the trial judge when the judge is offside, so be it. Usually, judges will respect counsel for standing up for their positions.

Most often, judges' questions arise after the conclusion of direct, cross, and redirect (if any). This is not a case of interruption. The judge has politely waited to see whether one of the lawyers will ask the question or line of questions. The judge wants to know something from the witness. Judges are aware that the lawyers do not have the same agenda as the judge. Perhaps this line of questions is one that both sides have studiously avoided. The judge's questions still represent information about how the judge is thinking.

Conclusion

LAWYERS SHOULD ACCEPT input from the judge for what it is, the communication of information. If the lawyer receives the information and learns from it, the lawyer can better prepare the balance of the case, but if the lawyer ignores such input, then the opportunity has been wasted.

CASE STUDY

IN A CASE where the insurer has denied liability in a disability claim, the following sequence of questions and answers occurs:

Q. Please describe how you came to complete the application for disability insurance.

A. My agent asked me several questions from the form, and then made a checkmark as I gave each answer.

Q. How did your agent deal with your experience with back injuries?

A. The agent asked the question, which I now read from the form itself, "Have you ever suffered an injury to the upper, lower, or middle back?" I told the agent that I didn't think so. The agent therefore put the checkmark under the "no" column.

Q. What discussion was there as to what constitutes a "back injury"?

TRIAL JUDGE. What does that matter? The witness saw the checkmarks, and the witness signed at the bottom. Each checkmark is initialled. That ends the matter, so far as I can see — please move on, counsel.

Draft a response for the lawyer to deal with the interrupting trial judge.

Solution

LAWYER. We submit that the duty of care requires more explanation than what was given by the agent. I understand that the witness will testify further about the discussion on this issue. From the pleadings, it is apparent that the back injury discussion is essential to this part of the claim. Such testimony should enable the court to deal effectively with this position. May it please the court that I pose the question to the witness?

When the Judge Does Not Get the Point

IF THE OBJECT of the exercise is to inform the trial judge, lawyers should change tactics when it appears that they are failing. Judges often let lawyers know that the information is not getting through, but often they do not. This leads to these questions:

1. How do lawyers know that there is a problem?
2. Once they know, what should they do about it?
3. If they suspect but do not know, what should they do about it?

There are always three possibilities when the judge does not appear to understand what points are being made:

1. The lawyer is incorrect, and the judge actually does understand.
2. The judge really does not understand.
3. The lawyer has not made any points, and there was nothing to understand.

How to detect the problem

JUDGES COMMUNICATE IN several ways. First and most frequently, they tell lawyers what they are thinking. Perhaps they do not follow the technical evidence, or perhaps they do not follow the logic that makes the evidence relevant or probative. In these cases, judges will express this to the lawyers. Judges also communicate with interruptions. They redirect the examination to other lines of questioning, and they rephrase the lawyers' questions to suit their line of thought. In these cases, lawyers can easily detect the disconnect between what they tried to accomplish and what they have accomplished. Sometimes, judges use body language to show discomfort. This is difficult to detect reliably, and, at best, any conclusion based on body language alone belongs in the "doubtful" category.

What should the trial lawyer do about this?

THERE IS NO obvious way to check when lawyers are not sure. They usually cannot ask the judge, "Did you get it, Your Honour?" If the uncertainty arises during the evidence phase, the lawyer can submit further evidence on the point. If possible, the lawyer can continue examining the same witness on the point. Rephrasing questions and coming at the point from another approach are the two choices available. The judge might say "Move on, counsel. I have heard this before." If so, there is little that the lawyer can do about it just then. Perhaps another witness can testify about the point later. The lawyer should ensure that the point arises in submissions, and then the lawyer can express the point and identify the relevant evidence. Perhaps such an explanation will correct the misunderstanding.

It may well be that the lawyer will recognize the uncertainty only during closing argument, when the lawyer expresses the significance of a point. Essentially, the lawyer has to do a better job of explaining the point, with references to the evidence adduced. To recite the evidence and logical sequence that demonstrates the point will present a challenge for the lawyer, who should proceed diplomatically, but firmly. Who wants to be shown to be slow on the uptake?

The lawyer should be accurate when presenting the point. Most judges will follow the presentation attentively, and if the judge still does not understand, there may be a further invitation to explain. If the judge understands but disagrees, the lawyer has to take that into account. Usually the judge will tell the lawyer where the point of disagreement lies, and if the point was important, this may cause a change in tactics. Often, the lawyer will simply have to concede defeat gracefully and move on to another point.

The question too many

THIS HANDBOOK STRESSES the risk of asking that extra question, the conclusion (or victory lap, as described in Chapter 5, below). The questions should have set up an inevitable conclusion. But perhaps the judge did not get the point, and the lawyer will regret not asking that final question? In this case, the lawyer should repeat the sequence of questions, hoping that the judge will follow the line to the intended conclusion. Now is the time for the lawyer to express the punchline out loud.

If there was no point at all

IN THE PREVIOUS situation, perhaps there was no point to be made. There is always the possibility that the lawyer is mistaken. Lawyers should constantly be guided by the possibility that the other person may be right, and that should be a humbling reminder for lawyers. The lawyer could reconsider how the point was made to determine whether it was successful or not. Bearing in mind that the point may have failed, the lawyer should consider how to make that point better or differently or whether to make it at all.

Conclusion

WHEN IT COMES to doubt, lawyers should acknowledge that trial judges are experienced lawyers themselves. They have several years at the bar to qualify for the bench, often in exactly the area of law that is involved with the present case. Lawyers can trust trial judges to get it right, because they usually do.

CASE STUDY

THIS EXCHANGE OCCURS in a case where the insurer has accepted a disability claim but has paid only 50 percent of what the claimant believes to be the correct amount. The following sequence of questions and answers occurs:

Q. How much did you earn from your job as a sales representative?

A. I was paid both salary and bonus, which was really a type of commission. My salary was $2,500 a month. My bonus was, on average, about the same amount.

Q. How often were you paid your bonus?

A. With every paycheque. I was paid my bonus based upon my previous quarter, divided by the number of pay periods.

Q. What deductions did your employer make from your paycheque?

A. The usual ones, which applied to both the salary and the bonus.

Q. How long had this been going on?

TRIAL JUDGE. What does that matter? The insurer paid the disability based upon the salary and not the bonus. So what if the employer did this for a long time?

Draft a response for the lawyer to deal with the interrupting trial judge.

Solution

LAWYER. We submit that the employer treated the bonuses as if they were part of salary. The deductions, which include employee contributions to the extended medical and disability insurance coverage, should have applied to both bonus and salary. The fact that this occurred over a sustained period suggests that the claimant was led to believe there was no difference between bonus and salary. Therefore, the claimant may well have expected the disability benefit to be calculated upon the two together. This expectation may form part of the contract, in our submission.

Who Is Your Audience (Hint: It May Not Be the Trial Judge)?

LAW STUDENTS ARE trained to anticipate that there will always be a trial to conclude a case. Even though alternative dispute resolution (ADR) is now taught as a compulsory subject in most law schools, the central tenet of lawyers' training is still that cases move inexorably from dispute to trial. Well, here is the spoiler alert: That is not the case. Almost nothing in civil court gets to trial, outside of small claims. Trial lawyers, except for those in criminal law, should change the name of their vocation. How does "settlement lawyer" sound? Hmmm, needs work. But the point is valid. Civil litigation is all about the settlement and no longer about the trial.

What does that signify for the answer to the question, Who is your audience in a trial setting? Of course your audience includes the judge, but who else is there? A great number of trials now settle after the first witness starts to testify and before the case gets to the verdict. Many cases settle after the last witness testifies and before the reserved decision comes down, or after the verdict and before the appeal is concluded. What this means is that the trial lawyer should pay very close attention to the impact of the case upon the opposing party and counsel. As preached in the handbook *The Civil Courtroom*, in this series, there should be as little friction between counsel as possible.

The personalities and behaviour of counsel should not present an obstacle to settlement — at any stage.

Both counsel and client who compose the opposing side should appreciate the significance of the evidence as it emerges against their position. They should be eager to settle the case in a manner that benefits them, which should benefit the presenting side as well. Where many years ago lawyers were taught to keep their cards close to the vest, now they are taught to make the significance of what is occurring obvious, apparent, and stark. The significance of a major point should not be buried in the fine print, to be disclosed as in the final act of a play. It may be true that the "butler did it," but this should be made known as soon as the clues are presented, and not be made obvious for the first time during closing argument. What is the point of "keeping your powder dry" if there is never an opportunity to shoot the weapon, due to a settlement before trial?

Perhaps in the context of criminal law, it is important to spring surprises during closing argument — not so in civil court, not after substantial sums have been spent on legal fees that could have been used to fund a deal. This cancels most need for subtlety. The best points are those that are not only made but are seen to be made. It is definitely the case that some points have to be kept secret until the commitment is made by an opposing witness or counsel, as is the case with previous inconsistent statements and impeachment opportunities. Nevertheless, in the civil trial setting lawyers should put their best foot forward early and often.

This means that the audience is not only the trial judge but also the opposing side (lawyer and client). There are several ways for lawyers to explain the significance of their evidence to the opposition. It can be done in submissions, in written argument, and even in correspondence between counsel. But lawyers should take great care to consider the positions taken by the opposition when they explain the significance of what is occurring.

Direct examinations are the scene in which most lawyers present their case. It may be appropriate for lawyers to load up the earlier part of the trial with their strongest witnesses just for the purpose of encouraging settlement on favourable terms. During cross-examinations, significant points may be made, and while the examiner may choose to avoid the question too many, pains should be taken to highlight the significance of the inference that a reasonable judge should draw from any given set of questions.

Conclusion

LAWYERS SHOULD PAY attention to more than just the pen of the trial judge. They should pay attention to the impact of the evidence on all of the players in this complicated stage production. Opposing counsel and clients have every bit as much of a role to play in settling cases as does the trial judge in deciding them.

chapter four

Direct Examinations

THERE ARE THREE types of examination that the trial lawyer will encounter. The first is the direct examination, in which the examiner examines a witness for the party represented by the examiner. The second is the cross-examination, in which the examiner questions a witness who is called by a party adverse in interest. The third is the redirect, in which the examiner gets to put questions to the witness that stem from answers given during the cross-examination. There is another type of examination, almost a hybrid of the direct and cross. This is the out-of-court examination, whether for discovery or by deposition, which is the subject of another handbook in this series, *Discovery Techniques*.

This chapter of the handbook canvasses the conduct of direct examinations. These are unlike the other two types in that the examiner can practise and prepare with the witness in advance. This suggests that there are three distinct phases to the preparation process:

1. The examiner prepares to interview the witness.
2. The examiner interviews the witness to prepare for the examination.

3. The examiner puts together the first two phases and prepares for the examination itself.

Each of these involves case analysis and preparation of an outline.

At trial, the examiner conducts the direct examination in real time. The purpose of the examination is to elicit evidence that will help the case of the examiner and hurt the case of the opposition. The examiner may want to either bolster the credibility of the examiner's witnesses or hurt that of the others. The examiner may also try to develop the back story and the theme or themes that will allow the examiner's position to prevail at trial.

The tactics that examiners employ during direct examinations are somewhat different from those employed during cross-examinations. There are constraints in how direct examiners may compose their questions, and there are opportunities for lawyers to prepare their witnesses for direct examinations, which do not exist for either cross-examinations or redirect examinations.

The preparation process can be the make or break point of the examiner's case. Not only does the examiner prepare the witness for the examiner's questions, but the examiner prepares the witness for the cross-examination that will follow. The first phase involves teamwork and storytelling, and the second, mitigation of risk and damage control. This chapter of the handbook canvasses all of these subjects.

Storytelling in Direct Examinations

THE DIRECT EXAMINATION is the opportunity for the witness to tell the story. Consider the commonly phrased question that begins, "Tell us in your own words . . . ." What does this mean? Does the witness recite from a script written by others? This section and the following one explore how the direct examination should allow the witness to tell the story.

The "story" is restricted to the components that the witness has to offer. For example, the witness may know about one part of the case but not others. That part should fit well into the overall storyline of the case, as presented by the direct examiner's other witnesses. This is where case analysis is so important. The function of the witness is to provide some of the components necessary for the direct examiner to make out the case. However, this alone does not make the testimony compelling, or even interesting.

Ability of the witness

THE STORYTELLING FUNCTION of a witness's testimony is very much a matter for the lawyer to consider. The relevant context is the capacity of the witness to tell the story. As with all examinations, lawyers should consider carefully the capacity of the witness to testify. This capacity includes the witness's ability to

- understand the question,
- appreciate its significance,
- articulate a response,

- moderate the response so that it deals with what the question asked, and
- defend the position in cross-examination.

This is not trivial as lawyers often ask questions that their witnesses cannot answer effectively, which does not mean that the witness is stupid. It does mean that the question may not match the capacity of the witness. This is a problem for the lawyer that can be remedied during preparation.

With respect to the storytelling value of the testimony, however, the lawyer should take into account what the case needs. This may transcend the case analysis, which focuses on the elements necessary to succeed. The storytelling function requires the lawyer to consider how best to present the elements in a compelling fashion. This is quite different from having the witness recite the elements and hoping for the best.

Themes

STORYTELLING SHOULD AUGMENT one aspect of case analysis: the theme. During case analysis, the examiner should spend considerable effort to properly frame the theme. The witness should use language and ideas that help develop the theme, because without this, the lawyer may not be able to do so. For example, if the theme of the case will be that the landlord chose to save money at the risk of tenant safety, then the witness should use language consistent with that theme: "cheap," "what would it cost?" and similar words or phrases, which should come from the witness before counsel uses them. Lawyers themselves may not be effective storytellers, but this does not mean that they cannot work with their witnesses to present the story in an effective manner.

Lawyers should make sure that the language of the question prompts the kind of answer that is required. For example, technically worded questions may provoke technically worded answers. Is this the intended result? This subject will be explored in more depth in the section "Teamwork With the Witness," below.

Timing

LIKE A GOOD joke, the secret to storytelling may well lie in timing. The witness should testify at the best time for the witness's part of the story and should testify (in chief) only for as long as the testimony supports the story. A small component of the case does not warrant a long testimony from the witness. The examiner can judge how long the witness should testify based on a combination of the significance of the testimony and the storytelling ability of the witness. With practice and preparation, lawyers can develop a good feel for this.

Conclusion

THE STORY HAS to be told by witnesses, and not by the lawyer. Even the best lawyer cannot create an effective story out of nothing. The best stories are those told by the witnesses themselves, and if the lawyer can weave the witnesses' stories into an effective and compelling development of the theme, the lawyer will have the best chance to persuade the audience.

Teamwork With the Witness

EFFECTIVE DIRECT EXAMINATIONS are the product of careful preparation. As has been discussed, preparation for witness examinations is a three-phase process:

1. The lawyer prepares for the interview.
2. The lawyer prepares the witness.
3. The lawyer takes what has been learned and prepares for the examination itself.

This section focuses on the relationship between the lawyer and the witness during the preparation process. Witness preparation is the subject of entire books. It is also the subject of ethical consideration, given the fine line between coaching and preparation. This section examines how a lawyer can tell the story effectively through the witness without crossing the line into coaching.

Lawyers should prepare themselves before seeing the witness. They should understand why the witness will testify and what is expected from the witness, and, at the same time, they should consider the vulnerability of the witness and how the witness can be exposed to cross-examination. Is the benefit worth the risks? With this in mind, consider the following formula to prepare a witness to be examined:

1. Can the witness understand the significance of the testimony? If so, the lawyer should brief the witness on where the witness's testimony fits within the overall story and should let the witness know what elements are required by case analysis. Witnesses do not testify from a script. It is important that they understand

why they are testifying and what significance their testimony will have. With this explanation, witnesses can understand where the lawyers' questions lead. This provides the general context.

2. From there, the lawyer should identify the areas that the lawyer will canvass during the direct examination. This is at a higher level than headlines. For example, the areas might be who the witness is, how the witness knows the parties, what happened in a few specific events, and what the witness knows about the impact of those events.
3. Within each area, the lawyer should prepare the witness to recognize the headlines and to answer the questions that follow the headlines. This will involve practice of the specific subjects for the witness's testimony. The headlines should lead the witness to tell the story, and a combination of open questions with full answers together with short open questions that follow up those full answers can develop the rhythm that makes any witness an effective storyteller. Headlines provide specific context.
4. Repetition is appropriate to review how the witness will perform. For example, the lawyer has asked the question, "What happened during the meeting?" and the witness gives a long answer that fails to cover one specific aspect. It is appropriate for the lawyer to point out what was missing and then ask the question again. But it is not appropriate for the lawyer to tell the witness the missing fact or the desired answer unless it is the witness who supplied the evidence to start with. Practice improves performance.

5. A common requirement for witnesses is that they supply the colour for a specific event, where the term "colour" includes adjectives, adverbs, and other evocative words that lawyers themselves cannot use during the course of their questions. Once the witness uses a colourful word, it becomes fair game for the lawyer during subsequent questions.

Warnings about rehearsals

IN THE PREPARATION process, lawyers face the risk that witnesses will appear to be rehearsed, wooden, or too smooth. The result is uninspiring and possibly not credible. Another risk is that witnesses may become too tense to do more than recite what they think they were taught to say. If they miss a line or two, they can freak out, and the result is a disaster. Lawyers should be mindful of the risks. If they detect that a witness cannot benefit from preparation, this reduces the effort that can usefully be devoted to the task. Witnesses should be encouraged to relax enough so that they appear natural.

The balance of power

IT HELPS FOR lawyers to tell witnesses that they know relevant things that the lawyer does not. This is especially true for experts, but it is often true for lay witnesses. This thought can empower some witnesses. Lawyers should watch out for opportunities to learn from the witness during the preparation process. They should be willing to ask what else the witness knows that may advance the case. The witness interview need not be limited to the facts or events. Perhaps the witness knows something about the other witnesses or about the theory of the case or about what happened after the relevant events ceased?

Coaching

COACHING IS FORBIDDEN by the rules of professional conduct. If a witness will say one thing in response to a question, the lawyer may not direct the witness to answer otherwise. But this is not to say that the lawyer cannot point out the consequences of such an answer. Witnesses can be told what will happen if they testify in a given manner. Spin is a different matter, and a witness who uses an extreme word or phrase or holds an opinion can be confronted with the weakness of that idea or opinion. However, when the witness testifies, it must be the witness who stands behind the truth of what is said.

One recurring nightmare of the trial lawyer is the witness who testifies, "But you told me to say that!" Lawyers should ensure that never happens. For some witness interviews, lawyers should bring a colleague or staff member to take notes. This provides the vulnerable lawyer with someone who can confirm that the lawyer did not lead the witness astray. That will save the lawyer's reputation should the nightmare become reality. Other sections in this chapter discuss hard questions, inoculation, and preparation for cross-examination, which are also essential components of the preparation phase.

Conclusion

WITH PRACTICE, THE lawyer and witness can develop the teamwork that is necessary to create an effective story and that makes the testimony an efficient process. Lawyers should be careful not to cross the line between preparation and coaching, and they should also be attentive to how fresh and spontaneous the testimony appears to be. If the testimony comes out as wooden or recited, it may lose all of the compelling value that the story requires.

Outline Preparation for Direct Examinations

THE SUBJECT OF outlines was canvassed in the context of examinations for discovery and depositions in this series's handbook *Discovery Techniques*. The concept is similar in the case of direct examinations. One major difference, however, is that the direct examiner gets to prepare the witness, which is not the case with discovery and depositions. When preparing for any direct examination, the lawyer should first consider case analysis. What does the case analysis require from this witness, including both the elements of the case and the theme language that will assist in persuasion? This is true for all witnesses in direct examinations but is especially true when dealing with the client.

There are cases where the client — as a witness — is a bit of a backwater. The client may be unable to testify due to age, infirmity, or possibly something that gave rise to the lawsuit, or the client may be a poor witness, being inarticulate, prone to exaggeration, or dislikeable. While usually the focus of the lawsuit, the client may not be a major witness.

The outline does not have to follow the elements in the case analysis. Often, the witness cannot contribute anything to some of the elements. The outline should follow some logical sequence that permits the witness to tell the story in the most compelling fashion. Because the lawyer gets to practise with the witness, the lawyer can work with alternative sequences of questions. The lawyer also gets to try out tactics with respect to inoculation against the anticipated cross-examination and can even set traps for the unwary cross-examiner.

The words used in each line of the outline should have as much detail as the examiner requires, but there are always trade-offs. If the lawyer has to write out each sentence, this will detract from the freedom to watch and react to the witness. On the other hand, if the outline contains only a couple of words per point, this puts the examiner at risk of stumbling over what to ask next. The level of detail of the outline therefore depends upon the experience and confidence of the examiner.

Any outline of a direct examination must account for the likelihood of cross-examination. This accounting should take the form of inoculation for those areas where the witness appears to be weak. The lawyer can weave the inoculation questions into the different outline sections, or, alternatively, it may be better to devote an entire section of the direct examination specifically to inoculation. During case analysis, the examiner will have considered the theme and elements of the case from the point of view of the opposition. This becomes critically important when preparing for inoculation. It may even determine whether the examiner should bear the risk of calling the witness in the first place!

EXAMPLES OF INOCULATION

Q1. The defence suggests that you were drunk at the time. What do you say about that?

Q2. The defence points to the Breathalyzer reading of over 0.08. How do you explain that?

Q1. The defence suggests that you already had a bad back even before the accident. What do you say about that?

Q2. The defence will likely refer to your visit to the doctor a month before your accident. The doctor's notes describe your back complaint. Tell us about that.

In the case of these two sequences, the outline may have only the two notations "Drunk" and "Pre-accident back," or it could contain far more detail. It is up to the lawyer to determine what works best.

Ideally, the outline will prompt the headlines of the direct examination. The outline with the headlines will form the basis of the trial judge's notes. Within each area, there should be headlines suggested by the outline's subheadings. Each sub-heading in the outline should easily translate into a headline, which the direct examiner can practise with the witness during preparation. The direct examiner must keep the witness in mind because the outline will fail if the witness cannot grasp what is asked. Each headline serves as a cue for the witness, who will expect the sequence of questions that follow.

The direct examiner should give specific consideration to how to use the witness as a weapon against the case analysis or theme of the opposition. Again, questions arising from this consideration can be woven into the body of the direct examination or may compose a separate section devoted exclusively to attack.

EXAMPLE OF OUTLINE

IN A TORT case, for example, the outline may include the following:

1. THE INTRODUCTION AND BACK STORY: There may be several topic headings that take the witness from relevant personal history to the facts of the case itself. Each sub-heading should easily translate into a headline.
2. THE LEAD UP TO AND THE OCCURRENCE OF THE EVENT: These headings will start with what happened shortly before the event and then will lead into the event itself.
3. THE CONSEQUENCES OF THE EVENT: The event occurred, and now what? Each heading here should deal with the after-effects of the event, whether at the scene or elsewhere.
4. THE PERCEIVED WEAKNESSES OF THE WITNESS'S TESTIMONY (INOCULATION): Examiners should anticipate how the witness will be cross-examined.

Conclusion

THE OUTLINE FOR the direct examination is an opportunity for the lawyer to implement the creative thought that led up to the trial. Litigators are not criticized for over-preparation. The preparation phase of the direct examination takes place in preparation time. The harder lawyers work on preparation, the luckier they seem to get at trial.

CASE STUDY

IN A CASE dealing with a slip and fall on ice, the witness is a neighbour who saw the buildup of snow and then ice on the path leading to the apartment building in the week preceding the accident. This witness will testify that the building manager put sand and salt on the path some days before the accident but took no action in the four days immediately preceding the accident. It snowed at least once three days before the accident. The witness saw several people, including a few residents of the building, slip on the path but did not see the accident itself.

Create an outline that would support the direct examination of the witness.

Solution

- Introduction
    - » Residence
    - » Proximity to building
    - » Observation of building
- History of snow clearing at building
    - » How often
    - » By whom
    - » How done
    - » Prompt for sand and salt
    - » Slips by residents and others
- Week before

- Last snow clearing
- Last sand and salt
- Prompt for by whom, when
- Slips there
- Pre-accident: days –4 to –1
    - » Last snow clearing
    - » Last sand and salt
    - » Prompt for by whom, when
    - » Slips there
- Inoculation
    - » Not able to observe constantly
    - » Failure to report deficiency to building manager or management

Headlines for Direct Examinations

BY NOW, IT should be clear that this handbook strongly supports the use of headlines. The function of headlines in direct examinations is different from that in cross-examinations. This section deals with the first of these two situations.

Each headline should serve as a neutral introduction to a subject. Headlines allow the witness (and judge) to understand the context for the questions that follow. They are not questions, and require no answers. In this respect, their use in direct examinations and cross-examinations is similar.

Headlines should avoid controversy, and they are not evidence. A controversial headline (often one that includes evocative language, such as "let's discuss the dangerous floor surface") will provoke an objection unless the evocative language itself has been adopted by the witness:

> Q. Please describe the floor?
> A. The floor surface was very dangerous.

> HEADLINE. We will now discuss the dangerous floor surface.
> Q. What was dangerous about it?
> Q. Why was this a danger?
> Q. To whom was it dangerous?
> Q. What could be done to reduce the danger?

As with cross-examinations, the headline should reflect the outline that the lawyer has prepared in advance of the examination. The lawyer who conducts the direct examination has had a chance to prepare the witness in advance, but this cannot be said with respect to cross-examinations. This difference matters.

Short sentences, simple language

TO PARAPHRASE THE formula used earlier in this handbook, headlines should involve simplicity. They should serve as direction markers, not as speeches. If the examiner cannot reduce the headline to a few words, the examiner does not get the point, and how can the examiner expect the witness or the judge to follow the train of thought? The "keep it simple, stupid" rule applies here. Keep the headline to a few words preceded by an introduction such as "let's discuss . . . ," "we will now discuss . . . ," or "I will now ask you questions about . . . ."

The headline should serve as the witness's audio cue to what part of the script will follow. Remember that witnesses are often very nervous and uncertain, and as the examination continues, they often tire. On the other hand, lawyers often appear to gain strength through the nervous energy created by performing onstage, and they may not feel their fatigue until the end of the day. This is rarely the case for witnesses — they feel it right then and there.

Headlines can serve as chapter breaks, with each headline closing the previous chapter and introducing the next one. The witness who has been properly prepared will follow the cue like a dance partner. Consider a novice actor who appears on a stage. How often would that actor appreciate a prompt or cue from the sidelines? The headline can serve this function. "We have now completed one section," the lawyer says, in effect. "Now we are going on to the next section." Implicit in this suggestion to use simple headlines is that the witness has been prepared to answer the questions that will follow each headline.

A word of warning about headlines

THE CONCERN OF many lawyers is that judges dislike witnesses who appear to be over-prepared. Judges want to hear witnesses testify from memory, and not from a script. On the other hand, those same judges may become impatient with witnesses who wander and who have not been prepared. Prepared witnesses are more efficient at delivering testimony on what matters. Most trial judges were trial lawyers before their appointment to the bench and know how the game works. They want to get to the heart of the matter as soon and as efficiently as possible. Most judges will trust counsel to get there in the best way possible, and if this means preparation of witnesses, it should come as no surprise.

In the case of cross-examinations, to be canvassed in the following chapter, the witness often makes some form of response that catches the lawyer by surprise. Witnesses try to hijack the cross-examination by using long or non-responsive answers. This should not be the case with direct examinations, where the lawyer has had the chance to prepare the witness. Further, the lawyer can phrase the question so as to encourage the type of answer that will best serve the situation, whereas in cross-examinations, the answer should be "yes" or "no" to virtually every question the lawyer asks.

Conclusion

LAWYERS SHOULD KEEP the difference between coaching and preparation firmly in mind. Headlines are definitely on the preparation side of that line. The headline is the connection between the outline prepared in advance and what the judge hears and records. A perfect outline will be reflected by headlines that incorporate virtually the same language used in the outline, and as such the perfect outline should appear almost verbatim in the judge's notes.

CASE STUDY

IN A PROFESSIONAL negligence claim made against an engineer for poor design of a building structure, the lawyer for the engineer wants to ask the engineer questions about the following areas:

- Experience of the engineer
- Contract with the building owner
- Purpose of the building
- Time constraints to prepare the drawings

For each, prepare a headline that will allow the lawyer to introduce the subject. There should be four headlines.

Solution

HEADLINE. Let's turn to your past experience.

HEADLINE. We will now discuss your contract with the building owner, your client.

HEADLINE. I will now ask you about the purpose of the building.

HEADLINE. Let's talk about the amount of time you were given to complete your job.

General to Specific

DURING DIRECT EXAMINATIONS, lawyers elicit information about all manner of events. The best way to procure this information from a witness is through initial broad open questions to which the witness supplies full answers. The direct examiner then follows up with questions that target specific subject matter. In this way, it is the witness and not the lawyer who tells the story.

The word "events" covers meetings, conversations, collisions, and everything that involves an occurrence. Even a thought can be an "event." With respect to most events, the witness rarely explains everything that the lawyer wants on record, and this is true even where there has been ample preparation.

Lawyers should not encourage answers that are very long, for a few reasons:

- Long answers may be difficult for the judge to follow.
- Long answers may depart from the subject matter sought by the lawyer.
- Long answers can detract from the quality of the story told by the witness.

Consider the interview in a news program, whether video or audio. The interviewer asks a question. If the person being interviewed answers for longer than a few sentences, the answer becomes more like a speech, and unless the person is both articulate and skilled as a presenter, the answer can be boring. Audiences tend to prefer that the answer be broken up with the give-and-take of an exchange between interviewer and interviewee.

The formula

THE MOST EFFECTIVE approach, therefore, is for the lawyer to ask a broad open question about the event: "What happened?" The answer should then be followed up with several targeted questions, all open, to elicit all the information that the lawyer wants about the event:

- "What was your reaction?"
- "What action was taken by X?"
- "Where was witness Y when this occurred?"
- "Tell me more about what the red card did?"
- "Why did you signal a left-hand turn?"

Effectively, the lawyer introduces the subject in a headline, the lawyer has the witness give an overview of the subject (event), the lawyer then leads the witness through specific components of the event that relate to the issues in the case, and the lawyer then moves on to the next subject.

Five-and-outs

REMEMBER THE FIVE-AND-OUT technique. It is common for the number of follow-up questions to exceed five, and if that is the case, the lawyer should consider a second headline within the same general subject. If the first question is about a meeting, the second headline could be about the role played by one person at the meeting, what resulted from the meeting, or something else. In each case, a new headline could elicit a general answer followed by several targeted questions.

EXAMPLE

CONSIDER THIS SEQUENCE of questions and answers in a typical direct examination:

HEADLINE. I understand that you met with the president on 3 August. Tell me about the meeting.

A. Well, the president had earlier asked me to come into the office to discuss my career. I was reluctant to do so, but attended because I was asked.

Q. Why did you think the president asked you that, at the time?

A. I know now, but I did not know before the meeting.

Q. What was the reason?
A. Because I was likely going to lose my job.
Q. How did the president approach that subject?
A. There was some discussion about the nature of the business, but it soon became apparent that my job was at risk.
Q. How so?
A. It was explained that we were losing customers. Cash flow was difficult. I was considered to be a luxury and not a necessity.

HEADLINE. I now want to ask you about your feeling of job security. What did you think the president was going to do?
A. Before the meeting, I had no idea.
Q. And during the meeting?
A. It became obvious that my job security was very much in issue.
Q. How so?
A. I was specifically told that if business did not pick up in the next few weeks, then I would be let go.

Direct examinations should have a rhythm, and this method permits the lawyer to proceed from event to event with a constant rhythm. This, in turn, permits the trial judge to keep up with what has been said. It also permits the lawyer to mark off those parts of the outline that have been accomplished.

This does not replace the art of listening for the direct examiner. Lawyers should pay very close attention to what the witness says. If the witness says something unexpected, for example, this may prompt a different type of follow-up question or another headline altogether.

When the lawyer changes the subject, the trial judge will know to ask any follow-up questions of interest before the lawyer moves on. From the point of view of the trial judge, the examination is also less boring because of the interchange between lawyer and witness. The judge quickly becomes accustomed to the timeout between the conclusion of one section and the beginning of the next, and if the judge is prone to intervene, the judge will know that an opportunity is coming up soon. This reduces the risk of a mistimed intervention that disrupts the lawyer's thought process.

This pattern of general to specific does not replace the art of watching the judge's pen. If the judge cannot keep up with the questions and answers, the lawyer might have to repeat questions or even full sequences, or the lawyer might have to ask the witness for further explanation. The lawyer should also pay attention to any quizzical look given by the judge or some sign of dissatisfaction, either of which may prompt the lawyer to change tactics.

Conclusion

THE GENERAL-TO-SPECIFIC METHOD is well-suited to allowing just the right amount of intervention by the lawyer to keep the story moving in the planned direction. It can be adapted to suit the sophisticated as well as the unsophisticated witness, and it can also be used as a tool to ensure that the trial judge keeps up with the information as it is provided. If the subject matter is novel for the trial judge, the direct examiner can fine-tune this method to provide greater depth of explanation.

CASE STUDY

IN A BREACH of commercial contract case, the buyer will testify about a meeting with the seller to discuss the number of units that the buyer needed. At issue are both the number of units and the extent of the buyer's urgency.

Create a headline for the direct examination with follow-ups to cover what is important. The outline should anticipate that the witness will ramble and not cover everything at first.

Solution

HEADLINE. I want to ask you about the meeting with the seller in which you discussed your requirements.

Q. Tell me about the meeting.

Follow-ups:

Q. How many units?
Q. Why so many?
Q. What did you tell the seller about that?
Q. How badly did you need them?
Q. What did you tell the seller about that?

Open, Closed, and Leading Questions

THERE ARE THREE basic types of question that lawyers ask during direct examinations. The most common of these should be the open question. However, a fair amount of experience is required to conduct an effective direct examination with open questions. What is the difference between the three types of questions?

- The open question is one to which the witness may respond in any way that the witness considers appropriate. The answer can be short, or it can be long — whatever the witness wants. An example is, "How did you leave the room?" Open questions almost always start with who, what, when, where, why, or how.
- The closed question is one to which the answer is restricted. The answer may be "yes" or "no," it may be "left" or "right," "up or down," or it may be any of "1," "2," "3," or "4." This type of question is quite permissible but is typically not designed to elicit much information. Examples are, "Which of the two doors did you take?" and "Did you exit the room via the door on your left?"
- The leading question is one to which the answer, either "yes" or "no," is suggested by the question. An example is, "You took the door to the left, correct?"

Note that each of the three types of questions might elicit an identical response: "I left by the right-hand door." However, only the first allows the witness the full freedom of response. Perhaps the witness did not leave by any door but rather left by the window, or perhaps the witness did not leave at all.

In direct examinations, witnesses should not be led except concerning non-controversial matters. This does not prohibit the lawyer from asking closed questions. The point is that the answer should not be suggested to the witness. So, which type of question is preferable for direct examinations? As with almost everything else that takes place in the courtroom, how to ask a question involves a judgment call: Is the subject controversial? Will the witness understand what information is solicited?

Examiners should ask their own witnesses open questions to allow them to answer questions freely, so long as they are comfortable with the subject matter. This increases the benefit of headlines with a limited number of questions for each headline. In direct examinations, the story should be told by the witness. Therefore the witness should provide the text for the story. However, the direct examiner is in charge of the agenda, and, generally speaking, the examiner should not ask witnesses wide-open questions that prompt lengthy answers. The plaintiff's lawyer should not simply ask the plaintiff, "Tell me the story about how you came to be injured." The examiner should break the subject into several topics, each with its own open questions.

Wide-open questions also reduce the degree to which the lawyer can control the telling of the story. Only very sophisticated and experienced witnesses can tell a story without much prompting in the way of questions from counsel. Consider too the trial judge. A steady rhythm of question and answer permits the judge to record the answer and listen to the question. One very long answer can be difficult for the judge to transcribe. Typically, the lawyer is more the master of the presentation of the story than is the witness. Again, headlines with questions and then answers on the subject followed by more headlines will present the story in a manner that the lawyer can ensure is acceptable to the trial judge.

If the lawyer intends to examine on a subject with which the witness is not familiar, the lawyer should restrict the questions to ones that will result in short answers. Closed questions may well be advisable in this case. Otherwise, the lawyer may venture onto unfamiliar ground, and this often leads to increased risk, which lawyers try to avoid wherever possible. But it may be necessary where there has been no preparation session with the witness.

Leading questions can be asked only in two circumstances during direct examinations. The first is where the subject matter is not controversial, and this will be covered in the section "When Leading Is Appropriate in Direct Examinations," below. The other allowable circumstance is where the witness has clearly forgotten what was recounted to the lawyer in preparation. The witness may have explained to the lawyer what the answer to the question should be, yet, for some reason, the witness has gone off-script. Perhaps the witness is giving unintentionally contradictory evidence or simply cannot recall. After a couple of prompts from counsel, most trial judges will allow counsel to lead the witness for that limited subject. Judges are experienced enough to give the appropriate weight to an answer suggested by counsel in these circumstances.

Conclusion

THE CHOICE OF question type should be intentional, and not a matter of default. Lawyers should not fall into the habit of using closed or leading questions because these are the easiest. True, the lawyer knows the answer that the lawyer wants to hear, but the lawyer should not use sloppy examination tactics to overcome a lack of preparation.

CASE STUDY

IN A WORKPLACE injury case, the supervisor will testify that the worker, AB, was not wearing a hard hat on the site that day.

Create three questions, one open, one closed, and one leading, to get that information.

Solution

Q. [OPEN] What was on AB's head at the site that day?

Q. [CLOSED] Was AB wearing a hard hat at the site that day?

Q. [LEADING] AB was not wearing a hard hat at the site that day, correct?

"What Happened Next?"

DURING EXAMINATIONS, LAWYERS ask questions about discrete subject areas. These subject areas are, for lawyers who prepare to conduct examinations, usually reflected by outlines that have been put in a sequence that best presents the evidence to the court. How does the direct examiner get from one subject area to the next?

There is nothing wrong with asking the simple question, "What happened next?" In direct examination it is common for a witness to testify about a sequence of events, where the testimony consists of one event followed by another event followed by another event. The simple question, "What happened next?" may well be the link that gets the lawyer from one area to the next.

With the proper use of headlines, there is little need for a segue from one section to the next. The headline serves as the break between sections. It indicates to both the witness and the judge that one area has finished and that the direct examiner is moving to the next area, which the headline identifies.

The outline for the examination may involve a chronological review of the events as they occurred. In other words, the outline could proceed from one event to the next to the next, and so on, and this could be somewhat boring. Lawyers should consider how to make the evidence a little more dramatic. This is not to say that the lawyer has to tell a great story with every witness, but it does suggest that the evidence should be as engaging as the circumstances will permit. "What happened next?" is not an entertaining way to present a series of events.

In preparation, lawyers can consider how to introduce the next subject once the earlier subject is completed. This may not be a simple task for the novice examiner to consider in real time, that is during the examination itself. Often, however, the lawyer moves off-script by reacting to answers rather than reading the next question in the outline. When this occurs, the simple question, "What happened next?" should be used to get the lawyer from point to point. It may not be entertaining, but it gets the job done.

There is another problem, however. The simple question may confuse or mislead the witness. What did happen next? Well, in the world of the witness, this may be an event that is not what the lawyer is looking to elicit by way of the testimony. The lawyer really wants to know what event that is relevant to the case occurred next. Therefore, the lawyer should consider the perspective of the witness to determine whether the next event from that perspective is the next event that the lawyer wants on the record. The best way to avoid the confusion is, again, with the use of the common headline.

In cross-examinations, the sequence of points follows a tight script, and the lawyer's questions fill the transcript. "What happened next?" is far too open-ended as a question to appear in most crosses.

EXAMPLES

Q. We have now completed discussion of that meeting. Now I'm going to turn to what you did immediately after.

This is one way to get the witness on to what happened to the witness. The witness may describe the trip home or a dentist appointment later that day.

Q. We have now completed discussion of that meeting. Now I'm going to turn to the next meeting.

This is one way to get the witness on to the next event that matters to the lawyer, rather than what happened to the witness. Lawyers should "lead" the testimony. The judge wants to know what happened that is relevant to the case. In that respect, the lawyer is very much in charge of choreography.

Both of these examples are headlines, and in both examples the examiner uses the headline to proceed to the next subject. The headline in both starts with a sentence that closes the previous subject area, which is not completely necessary. Lawyers could skip the first sentence of each of the examples and start with the word "now." The question for the lawyer is whether one method works better. That is a matter of personal choice.

This section is just a demonstration of headlines at work. They must be neutral, in that there can be no controversy. The headline cannot be used to suggest an answer and certainly not a controversial one. It should identify the new subject under discussion.

Conclusion

THE PURPOSE OF the examination is to impart information seamlessly to the trial judge. To accomplish this, the lawyer and the witness have to work together as a team, and this is best accomplished by the use of headlines and subject breaks so that lawyer, witness, and judge all know where the examination is going. With proper preparation, the witness can become accustomed to the rhythm of the examination. The pattern of headline, question, answer, and pause allows all three players to perform their roles efficiently.

CASE STUDY

IN A BREACH of contract case, a siding contractor is accused of installing the horizontal siding panels or strips on a house such that they formed a poor joint between the window and the strips of siding. As a result, the wind caused the siding to pull away from the side of the house, and moisture then penetrated the exterior walls. The direct examiner wants to ask the installer to describe the several installation steps. These are the steps, in order:

1. Install a J moulding adjacent to the window. This allows the siding to be secure to the window and to prevent water penetration.
2. Install the horizontal siding strips from bottom to top. This allows the overlap of horizontal strips to prevent gaps between them.
3. As each strip is installed, it must be securely fastened with nails or other fasteners at regular intervals. This prevents the strip from sagging.
4. Install the strip such that the edge of the strip is fastened very near to the J moulding. This prevents the strip from pulling away from the J moulding. Measurement of the strip is important to ensure that it butts into the moulding, as it is the secure butting into the J shape of the moulding that represents the "seal" between the strips and the J moulding.

Create a sequence of headlines and open questions that proceeds through the steps to allow the installer to explain the technique to the court.

Solution

HEADLINE. Let's discuss the proper method to install siding near windows.

Q. Please tell us what piece goes against the window.

A. We install a J moulding adjacent to the window.

Q. Why is that?

A. This allows the siding to be secure to the window and to prevent water penetration.

HEADLINE. So, we have completed the J moulding.

Q. What do you do next?

A. We install the horizontal strips.

Q. How?

A. We start to install the horizontal siding strips from bottom to top.

Q. Why?

A. This allows the overlap of horizontal strips to prevent any gaps between them.

HEADLINE. Well, please assume that you have installed the strips up to the base of the window.

Q. What do you do next?

A. Well, as each strip is installed, it must be securely fastened with nails or other fasteners at regular intervals.

Q. Why?

A. This prevents the strip from sagging.

HEADLINE. So we have installed the horizontal strips.

Q. What do you do next to attach them as you reach the windows?

A. We have to install the strips such that the edge of the strip is fastened very near to the J moulding.

Q. Why?

A. This prevents the strip from pulling away from the J moulding.

Q. What about the length of the horizontal strips?

A. Measurement of the strip is important to ensure that it butts into the moulding. It is the secure butting into the J shape of the moulding that represents the "seal" between the strips and the J moulding.

HEADLINE. So you have connected the horizontal strips to the windows through the J moulding.

Q. What is the next step in the installation process?

Preparation for the Hard Questions

DURING CASE ANALYSIS, the lawyer should consider carefully the case for the opposition, including the weaknesses in the case that the lawyer intends to present. These weaknesses are exploited during cross-examination by opposing counsel. In fact, this is one of the main reasons why case analysis includes the position of the other side. How can counsel mitigate these weaknesses during the witness preparation phase?

The weaknesses of the witness's testimony are the hard questions. In the initial interview with the prospective client, the lawyer may well have asked, "What will you say when you are asked this question?" And during the direct examination at trial, the lawyer should "inoculate" the witness against those hard questions that will be raised during cross, as will be discussed in the next section, "Inoculation." During the preparation phase, however, the lawyer has the time and privacy to prepare the witness to face those questions.

The problem often arises that witnesses (other than the client) see lawyers as the opposition. Lawyers may adopt the mantle of the devil's advocate, though this presumes that the witness has a weakness the lawyer can anticipate. The lawyer wants to work on that weakness so that it is minimized or, in the best case, turned into a strength. To accomplish this, the lawyer can simply put the question to the witness as the cross-examiner would put it. It can be put into context, with requests for detail and explanation. This should be the subject of careful preparation with the witness in advance.

Often, a skillful cross-examiner will put two facts together so that they appear to contradict each other. The direct examiner should try this tactic in the preparation phase. Perhaps one factual answer conflicts with another? Perhaps one answer will not be accepted due to other evidence that is more credible? There may be a third fact that should be conceded, there may be a way to reconcile what appears to be an inconsistency, or there may be a spin that could dampen the effect. All of these can be discussed so long as the lawyer does not tell the witness what to say. The witness stand is not the best place and cross-examination is not the best time for the witness to try to think up how to reconcile inconsistent statements or conflicting facts.

During the hard questions preparation, the lawyer may learn some hard truths about the case. These may cause the lawyer to choose not to call the witness at all or to try to settle the case on less favourable terms than previously demanded.

Conclusion

THE WITNESS WILL be exposed to cross-examination at trial. During the preparation phase, the witness should be exposed to as much of the cross-examination as possible so that the witness can be ready. Further, the lawyer should present the hard questions to the witness and work on how the witness will respond. In this way, the witness will improve in both confidence and performance.

CASE STUDY

IN A CAR-ACCIDENT injury case, the plaintiff did not wear the mandatory seatbelt, and in the collision, the plaintiff's head struck the windshield.

Create a headline and a couple of open questions to allow the plaintiff to give this testimony.

Solution

HEADLINE. I expect that counsel will ask you about your failure to use your seatbelt.

Q. Why did you not use it?

Q. What can you tell us about how the seatbelt would have protected you in this case?

Inoculation

WHERE A DIRECT examiner anticipates a likely subject for cross-examination, what tactics are available to reduce its effectiveness? Inoculation is a process that occurs during direct examinations, and its goal is to take the sting out of what will likely happen during cross-examination. It should be the subject of some preparation. This section explores the technique.

First, the lawyer must anticipate the thrust of the cross-examination. In case analysis, the lawyer should spend a great deal of time looking at the case from the point of view of the opposition. This arms the lawyer to prepare, during the witness preparation phase, for cross-examination by the opposition. At the trial itself, the lawyer can raise with the witness the anticipated cross-examination issues by way of inoculation. The typical lead up to this will be a phrase used by the direct examiner such as "My friend may ask you why . . . ." Of course, opposing counsel is not likely to start a question with the word "why," but this is the headline for an open question in response to which the witness will present the best spin possible on what should be a difficult area. When the cross-examination takes place and if that question arises, the judge has already heard the most favourable position of the witness on the subject. The novelty of the cross-examination point has been lost. In the best case, the cross-examiner will not raise the point, because it has been dealt with, effectively, during direct.

It may be argued that the opposing counsel will not raise the subject, so why should the examiner anticipate something that may not occur? There are several reasons for doing so:

1. The examiner should respect the ability of the opposing counsel.
2. The risk-to-reward ratio favours introducing the subject in a friendly way through the direct examination.
3. The direct examiner may not have an opportunity to redirect on the subject.
4. The answer can be rehearsed and practised so that what could be a difficult answer is presented in its best light. Cross-examiners do not allow the witness the opportunity to set the stage for how to answer. In the preparation phase, the lawyer should be careful not to coach the witness on what to say, but there is nothing wrong with rehearsing how it should be said.

Conclusion

INOCULATION IS AN excellent tactic to reduce the damage that lawyers anticipate from cross-examination. It can be practised in advance, it can be worked in a way that presents the evidence of a witness in the most favourable light possible, and it can reduce the dramatic impact that would otherwise result if a subject were raised for the first time during cross-examination. Inoculation is a mark of a professional examiner.

CASE STUDY

IN A DEFECTIVE car-repair case, the mechanic who made the repairs is accused of failing to conduct a brake inspection. The plaintiff's case suggests that any cursory check of the brakes would have detected the requirement for repair. The mechanic admits not conducting such an inspection but contends that this was not part of the mandate, which was to perform a wheel alignment.

Create a few open questions to inoculate against the suggestion that any mechanic should look at the brakes when dealing with the wheels.

Solution

Q. The plaintiff suggests that when you looked at the wheel alignment, you should also have checked the brakes. What do you say about that?

Q. What was your standard practice in that respect?

Q. Why was that your standard practice?

Q. [ASSUMING THE MECHANIC CAN GIVE OPINION EVIDENCE] How does that differ from the standard practice for mechanics such as yourself in this district?

Q. So in what circumstances would you have checked the brakes?

Anticipating Objections During Direct Examinations

OBJECTIONS CAN BE momentum killers. Just when an examiner is in full swing, up pops opposing counsel — "I object!" — and stops everything else. Worse still, the objection may be valid. There goes that line of questions. Ouch! One of the benefits of being able to prepare the witness in advance is that the direct examiner can identify where the testimony may lead to objections. In this circumstance, the examiner may work with the witness to reduce the risk that an objection will arise and if it does that it will succeed.

Most common objections can be anticipated during witness preparation, and some witnesses are sophisticated enough to understand the difference between what can and cannot be said in court. Where the witness tends to speculate or to offer opinions gratuitously, the lawyer should explain to the witness how to avoid this. This is also true for hearsay, although only very sophisticated witnesses can appreciate the significance of this rule.

Generally speaking, it will be up to the lawyer to lead the evidence of the witness to avoid the objection. As such, the lawyer can practise with the witness what information each headline solicits. If the witness responds with hearsay, speculation, or opinion, the lawyer can practise this area so that the witness can avoid those objections. During the direct examination itself, the lawyer should phrase the headline and the questions that follow in such a way as not to offend any of the rules of evidence. This is 100 percent within the lawyer's control. Often the lawyer asks a follow-up question that starts with the word "why," and with practice, a witness can learn what is and is not acceptable by way of response to such a question.

Consider the intended testimony. Does it conflict with an evidentiary rule, and how can the testimony be reconciled with that rule? This may require that counsel phrase the question as a request for fact rather than for opinion or for what the witness heard. This reflects the teamwork between the lawyer and the witness. A witness who has not met the lawyer before, much less practised the give-and-take of a direct examination, will often step afoul of the rules of evidence.

Conclusion

THE ANTICIPATION OF objections is a two-step process, and both steps require direction from the examining lawyer. The first step takes place during the preparation phase while the second step takes place during the examination with careful headlines and follow-up questions that the witness can answer without breaking the rules of evidence.

CASE STUDY

IF CORRECTLY ASKED, the witness will testify that the car seller warned the witness in a prior negotiation that the brakes required inspection and maintenance. The brakes later failed, causing an accident. Neither seller nor witness is a party. How can the witness be prompted to give the testimony without breach of the hearsay exclusion?

Create a headline and a few open questions to accomplish this.

Solution

HEADLINE. I will now ask a few questions about what you understood to be the condition of the brakes.

Q. What was your first experience with this car?

A. I tried to buy it from the seller.

Q. What was the result?

A. I did not buy it.
Q. Why not?
A. The seller warned me that the brakes needed repair. That threw me off, so I walked away from the deal.

"Please Explain" in Direct Examinations

DURING DIRECT EXAMINATIONS, it is not the lawyer who tells the story but the witness. The witness testifies to inform the court, not the direct examiner. As noted in the section "Who Is Your Audience," above in Chapter 3, sometimes the goal is for the witness to inform the opposition. It may well be that the lawyer fully understands what the witness has to say, but that is not the purpose of the exercise. It is imperative that the audience understands it as well. How is this accomplished?

During the preparation phase, the direct examiner implores the witness to use simple language. The lawyer uses short questions and simple language throughout the direct examination. Often, however, witnesses forget their instructions, or they do not have the capacity to follow this type of instruction. All too often, witnesses use jargon and long sentences with complex ideas. In this case, the most effective weapon of the trial lawyer is the common request "please explain," as illustrated in the following examples:

- The witness has just testified as to something that may be important: "Please explain."

- The witness has just testified as to something that may be difficult to grasp: "Please explain."
- The witness has used language that others may not understand: "Please explain." This is particularly significant with experts, many of whom are lost without their technical language.
- The witness may have just said something that apparently contradicts what has been said earlier: "Please explain."
- During inoculation, the witness admits to something that harms the case: "Please explain."
- This witness disagrees with what another witness has said or will likely say: "Please explain."

Repeated use of the words "please explain" can be annoying, and there are other phrases that get the point across. Examples include the following:

- "What do (did) you mean by that?"
- "Tell me more about that."
- "Why do you say that?"

The whole purpose of this exercise is to get the meaning across to the audience. If this requires explanation, so be it, and if this requires accents and highlighting, then this is how it is done. As soon as the lawyer asks one of these follow-up questions, the witness should provide a more detailed answer. During the preparation phase, the lawyer should warn the witness that this may happen. The witness's cue — "tell me more" or "please explain" — should lead to greater detail.

EXAMPLE

IN A TRIAL involving financial adviser negligence, the adviser testifies that the fixed-income component of the portfolio, as a percentage of the whole portfolio, should equal the age of the investor client. The following exchange takes place with the adviser (a party to the lawsuit):

Q. You used the term "fixed income." What did you mean by that?
A. Well, there is some controversy there, but what I meant was a type of security in which there is regular and predictable income spun off by the issuer.
Q. Okay, then. What is "income"?
A. Not capital growth or gains, but either interest or dividends.
Q. Companies are not compelled to pay dividends. How does that fit into your definition?
A. If a company has paid dividends every quarter for several years, then it becomes predictable and regular.
Q. How does the size of the dividends factor into this?
A. Nominal, tiny dividends, say below 1 percent, these don't represent income. The main idea behind owning these securities is their capital growth. But when there is a big dividend — today around 3 percent or more — then one main reason to own the securities is the dividends paid out, that is income.

Conclusion

IT IS UP to the lawyer to pay attention to what the witness has to say, and just as important is what impact that has on the audience. Where the effect can be improved with an explanation, it is incumbent upon the lawyer to ask for one. During preparation, the lawyer and the witness can form a team in which the words "please explain" lead to a persuasive answer.

CASE STUDY

IN A CASE where the insurer has denied liability in a fire insurance claim, the following sequence of questions and answers occurs with the policy claimant. The examiner knows that the daughter of the claimant has an adult boyfriend.

Q. Where were you the weekend when the fire occurred?
A. At my friend's cottage in the country.
Q. How long were you there?
A. I was there for just over a week.
Q. The insurance policy requires that you have someone, an adult, look in on your house every day if you are absent for a week or longer. What plans did you make for this contingency?
A. My children advised that they would look after this. One or the other would check on the house every day.
Q. How old are your children?
A. Well, my son was nineteen, and my daughter was seventeen.

Draft the next question for the lawyer to deal with the clause in the policy that requires inspections by an adult.

Solution

Q. The policy specifies that the inspections be carried out by an adult, which is eighteen years old in this jurisdiction. Please explain how it was that you directed your daughter to take on this task.

A. My daughter was then visiting her boyfriend, who was nineteen years old. He is a responsible young man. The two of them are now and were then inseparable. I knew that he would attend to this task with my daughter and that this would satisfy the terms of the policy.

When Leading Is Appropriate in Direct Examinations

EXAMINERS CANNOT LEAD the witness during direct examination (hostile witness excepted), or can they? There are several circumstances where it is appropriate for examiners to lead their own witnesses.

The first and most common circumstance is where the witness will testify about subjects that are not controversial. The following are examples:

- The biography of the witness
- How the witness came to know the parties
- How the witness came to be employed

It is acceptable to ask questions to make the witness comfortable with the practice of testifying, and it is also acceptable to lead the witness on these points to save time in court. Indeed, counsel may hand up a timeline or a curriculum vitae summarizing the information in documentary form.

Court time is valuable, indeed precious, and counsel should proceed through the non-controversial parts of the examination as quickly and efficiently as possible. This may require the lawyer to lead the witness through this information. But lawyers should still take the time to highlight the important points, even when they are not controversial. For example, it may be best for the expert to explain why a particular qualification is so universally respected or why the expert is better suited to opine than is the opposition's expert. Open questions are still best to accomplish this.

The other acceptable occasion to lead in chief is where the witness has struggled or may struggle to answer, which can be caused by nervous tension, by failure of memory, by language difficulties, or otherwise. It may arise because of the witness's personal circumstances. Also, leading children is common practice, and leading emotional witnesses is sometimes allowable. While it is certainly not ideal, the trial judge may specifically allow the lawyer to lead the witness on a specific point or at large. The judge is sophisticated enough to distinguish between evidence freely offered and that given in response to leading questions. Of course, except with children, any leading of the witness invites vigorous cross-examination.

Conclusion

LEADING IS COMMON in any direct examination, though it should be used judiciously. If a lawyer intends to cross the line by using it to explore controversial matters, it will require the permission of the trial judge. Otherwise, counsel can expect a vigorous objection.

chapter five

Cross-examinations

CROSS-EXAMINATION CAN BE the most dramatic part of the trial. It can also get the examiner into a great deal of trouble, and this is true regardless of how experienced the lawyer is. The fact is that the witness and the cross-examiner are usually adversaries, and the opposition witness has been prepared by competent counsel. Every question can result in a disastrous answer. Risks and rewards — that is what cross-examination is all about.

That said, there are effective techniques for cross-examinations. The first and foremost of these is that the cross-examiner has got to have a point. If the cross covers only the same ground as the direct, then the cross-examiner will have reinforced whatever message was communicated in the direct examination, and worse, the court will get the impression that the cross-examiner has nothing better to put forward. The formula for a successful cross-examination is for the lawyer to have a point, make the point, and get on to the next point. The effective cross will consist of a series of these points. Very few cross-examinations will have success followed by success followed by success. If it were that easy, everybody could do it. Junior litigators should spend a few days in trial courts just to watch how other lawyers struggle with cross-examination.

This section communicates several distinct ideas that will assist the junior litigator to get the job done. But all of the ideas are simply that, ideas. A litigator has to adapt any technique to the specific characteristics of the litigator. There should be a maxim taught to all trial lawyers: "Lawyer, know thyself." What works for one may not work for another, and what works in one circumstance may not work in another. Lawyers have to develop techniques that work for them; after all, it is the lawyer who is responsible to the client both for advice and for performance. This chapter of the handbook arms junior lawyers with some of the techniques necessary for successful cross-examinations.

Good Practices in Cross-examination

THERE ARE SEVERAL ways to skin a cat, and so, too, there are several ways to cross-examine a witness. This section will discuss a few of the good practices that cross-examiners should consider. As with other suggestions in this handbook, these are dependent upon circumstances and the lawyer conducting the cross-examination.

The first good practice is to use headlines. The lawyer should introduce each subject with a neutral introduction. This practice helps the judge to understand the testimony. It also allows the witness to follow where the cross-examiner leads and avoids interruptions to reorient the witness. In general, it avoids confusion.

Therefore, good practice is to make a list of the points that are appropriate for the witness and then figure out how to make these points, each point with up to five questions. Introduce each of the points with a headline. When the point is made, do not ask the question too many, which would allow the witness to give some explanation that would defeat the point. This requires case analysis, outlines, and discipline. Cross-examiners always have the option not to ask any questions at all. Once they start the process, however, they should make discrete point after discrete point.

Other good practices include these:

- Keep your questions short. This avoids confusion.
- Keep your language simple. This avoids misunderstanding and ambiguity.
- Stick to leading questions, not closed questions. A closed question can be answered in one of a finite number of ways ("left" or "right," "yes" or "no," "up" or "down") while a leading question should be answered in only one way. Here is an example: "Did you turn left or right at the T intersection?" This is closed. "You turned left, didn't you?" This is leading, as it compels a "yes" answer.
- Use pauses to maintain the desired momentum, and not speed of speech. This permits counsel to moderate the pace to accommodate the judge's pen. It also permits counsel to turn up the heat on the witness with little time between answer and next short question. Rapid speech risks losing

both the judge and the witness, and it may provoke an objection.

- Try to limit each question to one single fact. So if the witness strays, the cross-examiner knows where the disagreement lies. It forces the questioner to keep the questions short, and it also promotes creeping, described in the section "Beware the Trap," below in Chapter 5.
- Within leading questions, try to maintain one form of question to suggest that all answers are the same, all "yes." This develops a rhythm that witnesses may accept, causing them to agree with counsel even when the answer may require more thought.
- Use words that the witness has already used (a practice called looping). This avoids any confusion when the witness says, "Don't put words into my mouth. I never said that."
- Avoid using adjectives, adverbs, or evocative language until the witness has already adopted such language. This may be one of the many judgment calls that examiners must make. Sometimes, the cross-examiner wants to know what the witness believed: that the bridge was too far, that the car was travelling too fast, or that the speaker addressed the audience too softly to be heard. If that is the point of the question, then these words can be used, but the better technique is to make the modifier a separate question. Certainly the cross-examiner can suggest an evocative word to the wit-

ness. But better by far is for the witness to use it and for counsel to exploit such use.

- Creep up on a controversial subject. This allows counsel to abandon the subject upon running into resistance from the witness.

Consider this example of creeping:

Q. You were driving toward the intersection, correct?
Q. You were driving quickly, correct?
Q. You were driving very quickly, correct?
Q. You were driving faster than the speed limit, correct?
Q. You were driving dangerously, correct? (Note that this may well be the question too many!)

This example demonstrates the dreaded question too many and how lawyers can creep up on the point. The witness may resist any one of these questions by disagreeing with or balking at the answer. If so, the lawyer can then make the judgment call whether to ask the next question in the progression. The example also demonstrates how each progressive question, in this case, about driving speed can be added as a separate question. This would function equally well for any opinion of this nature. Here are some other examples:

- The bridge was far / very far / too far to reach in one day.
- The speaker was speaking softly / very softly / too softly to be heard.
- The dog was annoying / very annoying / so annoying as to be a pest.

Conclusion

THIS SECTION MAY have presented what would appear to be obvious techniques, but during the heat of a cross-examination, junior litigators would do well to remember them.

How to Tell a Story in Cross-examination

WITNESSES TELL STORIES, and counsel do not. At least, that is the theory. During the give-and-take of the adversarial system, the reverse can be true — counsel often become the raconteurs.

The outline of the cross-examination should be laid out so that the story can be told from the perspective of the cross-examiner's client. Whereas the direct examination encouraged the witness to tell a compelling story from the point of view of the party who called the witness, the cross-examination is a very different exercise. Open questions are rare, if they arise at all, and the text of the questions, framed properly, will result in a series of affirmative answers. Who tells the story if all the words come from the examiner and not from the witness? The one-word answers simply acknowledge that the story told by the examiner is correct. This requires a great deal of effort, thought, and creativity on the part of the cross-examiner. The outline should have a logical sequence that supports the story, but it does not have to be chronological. It can be broken down by issue, by event, or otherwise, to suit the story.

Remember the usual objectives of a cross-examination, the most common of which follow:

- Support the story of the examiner
- Attack the story of the witness
- Attack the credibility of the witness

If attacking credibility is the only goal, then there is no urgent need to tell a cogent story. If the examiner wants to tell the story, however, the logical sequence becomes just as significant as in the direct examination.

As with the use of outlines generally, the headlines should follow a sequence of points that the cross-examiner wants to weave into the story. Each headline should be followed by the punchline created by four or five leading questions. In effect, these punchlines tell the story.

Conclusion

IF THE CROSS-EXAMINER has been completely successful, then the series of punchlines coming from each of the subjects can be used verbatim in the closing argument. That is how to tell a story.

CASE STUDY

IN A BREACH of contract case, the home builder sues the supplier of timber that was intended to serve as the structure for the homes in a subdivision. The builder's lawyer wants to present the story that the supplier was aware that its client depended on timely delivery but disregarded the client's interest. The supplier promised ample supply on a timely basis without first securing its own supply lines. When the wholesale supply chain tightened up, the supplier chose to delay the delivery instead of paying higher prices to its supply source.

Create the outline of a cross-examination of the supplier to tell this story. The idea is that each point in the outline would become one or more five-and-outs to make the point. Put them in an order that makes sense as a storytelling exercise.

Solution

- The supplier was knowledgeable about lumber supplied for use in home construction.
- The supplier persuaded the builder to rely on the supplier.
- The supplier priced the supply contract to earn a profit.
- The supplier failed to secure its own supply.
- The supplier trusted its ability to get timber as needed.
- The wholesale market in which the supplier procured its inventory tightened up.
- This drove up wholesale prices.
- If the supplier had bought at these new prices, its profit margin would have dropped.
- The supplier declined to supply the builder on time.
- The supplier knew its decision would cause delays for the builder.
- The supplier knew these delays would damage the builder's business.
- The supplier knew its delays breached its promises made at the outset.

Point-First Cross-examination

ONE OF THE basic rules of legal writing is that the author should make the point first. The author should make the point at the beginning of the article or the paragraph — make the point first. How does this work in cross-examination?

For the most part, "point first" does not belong in cross-examination. The logical sequence of the cross-examination should be designed in the preparation phase to make the points in an order that will make the most sense to the audience. This may well involve a series of points leading in a crescendo to the concluding point. It may be a chronological sequence or a sequence broken down by issue. Whatever the case, point first does not belong.

There are, however, a few circumstances in which the cross-examiner will want to lead with the strongest point first:

1. When the direct examination has made a specifically dramatic point. If the cross-examiner can diffuse that point easily, that may well be the first point to make in cross.
2. When the success of the cross-examination depends on one single point. Perhaps the cross-examiner must establish that the witness was not at the scene of the event, or perhaps the cross-examiner wants to establish that the witness cannot recall nearly as much as the witness has testified to in chief. Whatever the reason, if everything depends upon one point, the lawyer should make that point the focus

of the cross-examination. This may require that the lawyer lead up to the point with careful background points made along the way, or it may require the cross-examiner to make the point first. In all examinations, the examiner should structure the outline so that each point makes sense within the sequence of the examination.

3. When the trial judge is not familiar with the area under discussion. The sequence of the cross-examination should be adjusted to educate the trial judge, which may require that the most important point is made first and that the other points are used to support the conclusion.

Conclusion

THIS IS AN example of where legal writing and the question and answer of cross-examination are not analogous to one another. However, the cross-examiner must keep in mind that the points made on cross-examination are to be used during closing argument, and that is where point first truly belongs.

Bad Practices in Cross-examination

WHEN THINGS GO wrong during cross-examination, it may well be the result of poor technique. The section, above, on good practices is now followed by this section on poor practices. Why did the cross-examiner fail to make the intended point? Here are the usual suspects:

- The question was vague. It did not narrow the subject to one that the witness had to answer on point.
- The question was ambiguous. It allowed the witness to choose how to answer the question, and the witness did not choose the answer that the lawyer had expected.
- The question contained two questions. The witness did not understand which question the lawyer had meant or chose the one that the lawyer had not meant to ask.
- The question used technical language. The witness either genuinely did not understand or pretended not to.
- The question went on too long. The witness forgot the point or got lost in it. When this happens, the judge may show great sympathy for the witness.
- The question mixed negative with affirmative. By answering "no," the witness agrees with the suggestion posed by the question. For example, the correct affirmative answer to the question, "You did not do that, do you agree?" would be "Yes, I agree I did not do that." This is very confusing to the witness and the judge.
- One question did not follow the previous question, or the answer. Without a headline, the witness (and the judge) may not be able to follow what the point is, and if the lawyer changes the subject without notice, this can confuse the audience.
- The lawyer argued with the witness. The lawyer disliked the answer and chose to pick a fight. Well, the technique is called "five-and-out" for a reason:

the "out" applies when the lawyer has made the point, or cannot do so quickly. The cross-examiner should move on to a point that can be made.

- The answer was responsive but did not make the point the lawyer wanted. Here, the outline failed to connect the dots between the headline and the point.
- The question let the witness off the hook. Perhaps the cross-examiner had succeeded on a major point. But if the examiner then put the point in play again, that may well have been the dreaded question too many.

Conclusion

NOT ALL QUESTIONS in cross-examination will succeed in making the sought-after points — far from it. And for those that fail, the cause may be poor technique. For all of the poor techniques listed above except for the last one, the prescription is the same: Headlines. Simple language. Short questions.

CASE STUDY

IN A SLIP-AND-FALL case, the plaintiff victim is asked the following initial questions about the snowfall that blocked the path, with the numbered questions (Q1, Q2, etc.) coming after:

Q. When you entered the house, it was in daylight, correct?
A. Yes.

Q. And there was no snow on the walkway, correct?

A. Yes.

Q. Or ice?

A. Correct.

Q. You knew a lot of snow was expected to fall, correct?

A. Yes.

Q. And you could see the snow falling from your vantage point in the dining room, correct?

A. Yes.

Q1. So what did you see when you left?

A. What do you mean?

Q2. You could not get out the front door, could you?

A. It was not locked, if that is what you mean.

Q3. Did you put on your boots and head out?

OBJECTION. I object. That is two questions.

Q4. You knew from the predicted orographic precipitation to expect that snowfall, correct?

OBJECTION. I object. What does THAT mean? [Hint: look it up.]

Q5. Well, when you decided to leave, you knew that the weather was awful, that walking might be treacherous, and that the area was prone to sudden snowstorms with big snowfalls. That caused you some concern, correct?

A. I am sorry. What are you asking?

For each of the numbered questions, rephrase it to make it sensible.

Solution

Q1. When you opened the door to leave, what did you see on the walkway?

Q2. [BEST POSED AS TWO QUESTIONS] There was a large amount of snow, correct? Yes.
And it blocked your exit, correct?

Q3. Did you then put on your boots? Yes.
And then you headed out, correct?

Q4. You lived near a mountain, correct? Yes.
And you knew that mountains can lead to big snowfalls, correct? Yes.
And it happened there from time to time, correct? Yes.
And you heard that this was predicted for that evening, correct?

Q5. [HEADLINE] Let's discuss what you were thinking as you went to leave.
You knew the weather was bad, correct? Yes.
And that big snowfalls occurred there? Yes.
Several times a year, correct? Yes.
And that snowfalls make for dangerous walking, correct? Yes.
That concerned you that evening, correct?

Victory Laps (Often, the Question Too Many)

THE LAWYER HAS made a point in cross-examination. That should be where the point ends, at least for the moment, and any further reference to it during that examination becomes unnecessary, redundant — in poor taste, really. And worse, it becomes an unnecessary risk. This is the victory lap, analogous to the post-win lap around the track taken by the speed skater or car racer, a big smile displayed to admiring fans. Once a lawyer has embarked on a mission to accomplish a point, it is the testimony that makes the point. A successful five-and-out exercise will make the point without the lawyer actually expressing it. If the lawyer then expresses the point, there had better be a good reason for it, discussed in "Attack Mode," below in this chapter, as it risks asking the question too many.

Counsel may weigh the risk-to-reward ratio of a victory lap where the audience appears to have missed the point, whether the audience is the judge or the opposition. The victory lap is often a rhetorical device, a repetition of words just used by the witness. But not only is it usually unnecessary and impolite, it comes with a risk because once the witness appreciates the significance of the testimony, the witness may try to get out of it. Even where the lawyer cannot see how the witness can escape the trap, witnesses often manage. Counsel should not give the witness the opportunity to do so.

In this series's handbook *Discovery Techniques*, this situation is canvassed in some detail in the context of discovery. Perhaps the lawyer has just procured an excellent response from the witness. Does the lawyer give the witness an opportunity to explain? In discovery, the lawyer may choose to do so fearing that the answer will be raised at trial, and to be prepared for trial, the lawyer wants to hear the full answer right then and there.

In cross-examination, however, the consideration is totally different. The only opportunity that the witness has to explain may well occur during redirect examination. The cross-examiner should therefore think of the question, as raised in "Beware the Redirect Examination," below in this chapter, Will the lawyer who called the witness ask the question on redirect, and allow the witness to explain? As with so much in cross-examination, this calls for judgment on the part of the cross-examiner.

Conclusion

THE SAFEST TIME to employ the victory lap is when the witness is off the witness stand and when the lawyer is in the middle of closing argument. There is then no chance for the witness to offer the possible explanation. If opposing counsel does so, it will be without the benefit of what the witness would have said had the question too many been asked during the cross-examination.

Bad Answers in Cross-examination

WHAT CONSTITUTES A bad answer in cross-examination? There are two types of bad answer. The first is one that simply does not respond to the question. Consider this sequence:

Q. What colour was the barn?

A. It was very high.

The witness does not intend to annoy or misbehave. The witness simply did not get the question, and this may not be the fault of the witness. Consider this sequence:

Q. Where did the defendant strike you?
A. Near the garage.
Q. Let me rephrase. Where on your body did the defendant strike you?
A. Oh, on my leg.

The other type of bad answer is one in which the witness acts intentionally to thwart the purpose of the examiner. There was nothing wrong with the question, but the witness is trying to fight back. Consider this sequence:

Q. So you admit that you were in a hurry?
A. I never said that.
Q. Well, I put it to you that you were in a hurry. Correct?
A. I never said that.

In both cases, the initial technique should be to pose the question again. If the witness did not understand it, then the question should be rephrased: headline, simple language, and short question. Often, the trial judge will also be confused, either by what the witness answers or by what the question asked. Rephrasing is always a good policy in this circumstance. If the witness is behaving as an adversary, then putting the question exactly as it was initially asked is a fair tactic. Yes, the lawyer who called the witness can object, "Asked and answered." Nevertheless, asking the question again will make the point that the answer was non-responsive.

What happens next will depend upon the answer or if there was an objection the reaction of the trial judge. The answer could repeat the previous non-responsive one, and in this case, it becomes a battle of wills between the cross-examiner and the witness. If the cross-examiner genuinely wants to deal with the point, then the tactics must change, and the point should be approached from a different angle. The examiner should create another headline and up to five pointed questions to get the point across again.

EXAMPLE

THIS IS A continuation of the last question-and-answer sequence above:

Q. So you admit that you were in a hurry?
A. I never said that.
Q. Well, I put it to you that you were in a hurry. Correct?
A. I never said that.

HEADLINE. Well, let's discuss what was going through your mind then.
Q. You had an appointment, correct?
A. Yes.
Q. And you had to drive all the way across town, correct?
A. Yes.
Q. You thought you would be late, correct?

It does not matter what is answered at this point. The cross-examiner has made the point, successfully. The unspoken punchline is that the witness was in a hurry.

Conclusion

THE CROSS-EXAMINER SHOULD never argue with the witness, as that will surely provoke judicial intervention, or at least a well-deserved objection. The cross-examiner should make the point in a manner that is clear and concise. This will expose whether the witness is misbehaving, and it will often get the desired answer.

CASE STUDY

IN AN ASSAULT case arising from a bar fight, the five-foot-two-inch, slender bartender is asked in cross-examination about why he did not try to prevent the fight:

Q. So you heard the raised voices, correct?
A. Yes.
Q. Right in front of you, correct?
A. Yes.
Q. And you did nothing to intervene, correct?
A. Do I look like a bouncer?

Create a headline and a few leading questions to deal with this non-answer.

Solution

HEADLINE. Let's talk about what you did not do at that point.

Q. You did not try to get the attention of either patron, correct?
A. Yes.
Q. You did not call for a bouncer, correct?
A. Yes.
Q. Or a manager, correct?
A. Yes.
Q. Or the police, correct?
A. Yes.
PUNCHLINE. [UNSPOKEN] You didn't do anything that was reasonably in your power to deal with the situation.

Attack Mode

IN THE ADVERSARIAL system, cross-examinations are not meant to be gentle. It is expected that a vigorous cross-examination will involve some level of confrontation between counsel and witness, but this does not require rudeness, or lack of civility. It may, however, require that the cross-examiner push the witness around somewhat. What does this mean, what will it entail, and what are the limits?

Examiners should always operate according to their personality. That said, there are often hard questions that counsel will direct to witnesses in cross-examination. Cross-examiners should remember that it is not they who pass judgment upon the witnesses and that it is their job to raise the points from which others can draw conclusions. Therefore, the cross-examiner should usually not express an accusatory conclusion. The question too many usually involves the cross-examiner's putting exactly this kind of conclusion to the witness. Who appointed the cross-examiner as the judge?

Consider the following sequence of questions, to which each answer is "yes."

HEADLINE. We will now discuss what happened in the stockroom that day.

Q. You entered the room, correct?

Q. The floor was wet from melted snow, correct?

Q. You had access to a mop nearby, correct?

Q. Your job duties included cleaning the floor, correct?

Q. You did not clean up the floor then, correct?

This is a very aggressive set of questions. The conclusion (unspoken punchline) is that the witness was derelict in performing basic job duties, and the inference is that the examiner has accused the witness of a dereliction of duty. But this accusation remains unstated. It is up to the judge to connect the dots, to reach that conclusion. It is not up to the cross-examiner.

When to ask the question too many

IT IS ONLY good practice that prevents the cross-examiner from putting the ultimate question in the sequence to the witness. In the sequence of questions in the example above, that question might be, "You didn't do your job, then, did you?" This may provoke the witness to defend the merits of the conduct. Why take the risk that the explanation will let the witness wriggle off the hook? Here are some possible reasons:

- The cross-examiner may want the explanation to make it plain how weak it really is.
- Perhaps the explanation is not as strong as an alternative theory, as explained by another witness.
- Perhaps the cross-examiner wants the explanation early in the examination so that it can be destroyed later.
- *Browne v Dunn* (to be dealt with below, in this chapter)

Conclusion

A SERIES OF headlines and short sequences of questions can be devastating. It is aggressive. It is attack mode at work. The cross-examiner can change tone of voice, pace of speech, pauses between answer and question, and loudness to modulate the level of aggression. This is as important to suit the character of counsel as to suit the situation.

CASE STUDY

IN A FAMILY law case, the cross-examiner wants to make the point that the witness abandoned the infant for an hour to run chores, while the witness was responsible for the infant.

Create a headline and a few leading questions that suggest culpability by the witness.

Solution

HEADLINE. I will now ask some questions about what happened that afternoon.

Q. The parents left you in charge of the child, correct?

A. Yes.

Q. At their home, correct?

A. Yes.

Q. And you left the home, correct?

A. Yes.

Q. To run some chores, correct?

A. Yes.

Q. And left the child at home, correct?

A. Yes.

Q. Alone, correct?

A. Yes.

Q. For an hour, correct?

A. Yes.

PUNCHLINE. [UNSPOKEN] You abandoned your post for a trivial reason.

Friendly Mode

IN CROSS-EXAMINATION, NOT all witnesses are adversaries, and for those that are, they may not be adversaries in everything they have to say. In cross-examination, lawyers should distinguish between adversarial and non-adversarial circumstances. How does this work?

Remember that there are three common objectives in any cross-examination:

1. Build your case.
2. Teardown their case.
3. Destroy the credibility of the witness.

The witness may be able to assist in the first two and may also be able to help build or destroy the credibility of someone else. When this opportunity arises, counsel should be prepared to switch from attack mode to friendly mode.

Essentially, the witness becomes the ally of the cross-examiner, who then gets the best of both worlds. First, the cross-examiner gets to lead the witness, and second, the witness will be pleased to follow that lead. The formula for success remains in place: headlines, short questions, simple language. The outline will identify where the witness is helpful. The cross-examiner may choose to switch into open-question mode as if this were a direct examination. The cross-examiner should act in a way that allows the witness to tell the story in the most effective manner.

It may well be that the witness said something in the direct examination that caused the cross-examiner to expect friendly evidence. The prepared outline for the cross-examination can turn into an outline for a friendly direct examination easily enough. The five-and-out system allows for a simple conversion: keep the headlines, and turn the questions into open questions. Alternately, ask the leading questions in a slow and friendly manner, seem to invite longer answers, and allow lots of time for the pause between the witness's answer and the next question. But be prepared to follow up with short, targeted open questions.

If the witness has both adversarial and non-adversarial evidence to give, be prepared to ask about the non-adversarial subjects first. Adversarial witnesses do not suddenly change sides in the course of their testimony, and this may be as much a question of how they want to behave as it is a question of what answers they give. It will be easier to lead a willing witness before animosity arises from the attack mode questions, which are best directed at adversarial witnesses.

An alternative approach is to mix attack mode and friendly mode. Witnesses may feel a sense of relief when attack mode ends, and respond well to friendly mode. Lawyers themselves can use this as an opportunity to regroup, to marshal their own resources. Attack mode can be stressful to lawyers as well as to witnesses. Stress leads to fatigue, and fatigue leads to mistakes. Friendly mode causes less wear and tear on the cross-examiner.

There are other circumstances where friendly mode is the best way to proceed. Here are some examples:

- The lawyer's specific preferred method of approach to witnesses is friendly. This can be described as the "parlour room" method, where the lawyer chats with the witness to develop a rapport, which is then used to encourage the witness to help get to the truth in a co-operative manner. Imagine that the lawyer and the witness are sitting in armchairs in a residential living room and that although the lawyer leads the discussion, it is very much a two-sided affair.

- There is something about the witness that forces the lawyer to use a soft examining style. Perhaps the witness is particularly sympathetic, as discussed in "The Sympathetic Witness in Cross-examination," below in this chapter, or perhaps the witness cannot be cross-examined because of age or disability.
- The lawyer senses that the trial judge is particularly partial to the witness, something that can emerge either from the direct examination or from earlier parts of the cross-examination. Many trial judges give signals with respect to their tolerance for harsh cross-examination tactics, and lawyers should be on the lookout for such signals.
- The lawyer needs to build a base of testimony upon which to conduct an adversarial cross-examination later. Where there has been an examination for discovery or deposition beforehand, this requirement for a foundation would be unusual. Where the witness has not been subject to some form of transcribed examination in advance of the trial, the lawyer may require some level of foundation before switching to attack mode. This may be handled best with open questions and a gentle demeanour.
- Some lawyers simply cannot deliver an effective cross-examination using the attack mode. Either they feel that their personality is not conducive to such an approach, or they are otherwise inhibited.

Conclusion

IN MANY CASES, the cross-examiner can anticipate the witness who will be non-adversarial, at least in part. If so, the examiner can prepare for this during the preparation phase. The outline could reflect the non-adversarial questions, but the general thrust of the outline remains unchanged. The lawyer still wants to accomplish the objectives of the cross-examination.

CASE STUDY

IN A CONSTRUCTION case, the owner hired an architect to supervise the job site. The contractor sues the owner for the price of work performed on a building extension on the project. The architect testifies in chief that the work on the extension was authorized by the owner and was not covered by the base contract. The work on the main building was all covered by the base contract price.

Create a headline and a few questions — leading or not — to deal with the extension.

Solution

HEADLINE. I will now ask a few questions about the extension.

Q. The base contract covered the main building, correct?

Q. What about the extension?

Q. How was work on the extension to be valued?

Q. What was your role in authorizing it?

Q. When was my client to be paid for it?

Beware the Trap

TRAPS ARE COMMONPLACE in cross-examination. The witness is typically the adversary of the cross-examiner, and in cross, witnesses usually want to show up counsel. If the cross-examiner wants red, the witness wants black. Effective direct examiners may anticipate where the cross-examination will go. This leads to the subject of traps.

The trap is simply the situation where the witness has a killer answer for the cross-examiner's next question. This may be set intentionally. The direct examiner may not ask the question specifically so that the cross-examiner will fall into the trap, unprepared, and that the answer may become more devastating. The trap may also arise by accident. The witness may simply have a great answer for that question. In both these circumstances, how can the cross-examiner avoid making a terrible mistake?

The easy solution is that cross-examiners should never ask a question to which they do not know the answer, and if they receive an answer that is contrary to what they know, they can impeach the witness using reliable contrary evidence. However, that is much easier said than done. Cross-examiners usually have to take some risks to accomplish their objectives.

As cross-examiners, you should remember and follow this mantra: "Simple language. Short questions." Now, add one more element: "Creep up on the subject." If the cross-examiner asks for a conclusion or an opinion, the cross-examiner must live with the answer. Therefore, open questions are to be avoided, unless the answer cannot possibly cause harm or unless there is no alternative. On the other hand, if the cross-examiner asks several short leading questions, it is possible to creep up on the subject, and the subject can be cut short at the first sign of danger.

EXAMPLE

CONSIDER THE PUNCHLINE question, "You were not paying attention, were you?" This conclusion can be accomplished with less risk by creeping, in a manner that is just as effective as if the witness answered "yes" to the punchline question about not paying attention.

HEADLINE. I will ask you about your drive that day.

Q. You were driving the family to hockey practice, correct?

Q. Your son was in the front seat, correct?

Q. Your daughters were in the back seat, correct?

Q. They were talking, correct?

Q. And so were you, correct?

Q. The radio was on?

Q. Music was playing?

Which of the two choices is better? Creeping up on the subject or asking the punchline question? The inference one draws from the headline and sequence of short leading questions is that the witness was multi-tasking and was therefore distracted. This is inescapable. The punchline question should not even be asked, as the witness may be ready to give an effective answer. This avoids the potential trap.

Conclusion

ESSENTIALLY, CROSS-EXAMINERS MUST be attentive to all risks when asking questions. As with much of the practice of advocacy, cross-examiners constantly face a risk-reward challenge. If a cross-examiner asks the next question, the answer may damage the case. Any question asked may be the dreaded question too many. But by creeping, the cross-examiner can change the subject before getting into real trouble. Creeping requires headlines with short questions and simple language, and that the cross-examiner be alert to the possibility of traps.

CASE STUDY

IN A CHILD custody case, the witness has testified that the mother's home is located on First Avenue, several blocks from the school on Ninth Avenue, which the parents had chosen for the seven-year-old child. This is four blocks — all side streets — farther than the father's home on Fifth Avenue. The cross-examiner is the lawyer for the mother, and this lawyer is fearful that the witness will have a damaging answer to the punchline question, "The extra distance is no big thing, correct?"

Create one or more headlines and some leading questions to achieve the punchline by creeping up on it.

Solution

HEADLINE. We will now discuss the location of the mother's house.

Q. It's on First Avenue, correct?

A. Yes.

Q. Eight blocks from the school, correct?

A. Yes.

Q. About a ten-minute walk to the school, correct?

A. Maybe for an adult.

Q. And a five-minute walk from the father's home, correct?

A. I guess so.

HEADLINE. Now let's talk about how the child should get to school.

Q. An adult would always accompany a seven-year-old to school, correct?

A. Of course.

Q. Or they could use the school bus?

A. If you say so.

Q. In which case the extra distance of four blocks does not matter, does it?

A. I suppose not.

Q. And a ten-year-old can walk to school alone, correct?

A. Yes.

Beware the Redirect Examination

THE CROSS-EXAMINER SHOULD keep in mind that the direct examiner has another kick at the can. This is called redirect examination, and it allows the direct examiner to clear up anything that arose during cross-examination. It is significant for cross-examination because some judgment calls arise that will be decided based upon anticipation of the redirect.

If the cross-examination makes a point, sometimes the witness will say, "May I explain?" The cross-examiner then has a choice. If the witness gets the chance to explain, the cross-examiner will have lost control of the examination. Who knows what the witness will say? On the other hand, if the cross-examiner refuses the request, then the redirect examiner may well invite the witness to give that explanation: "On cross-examination, you offered to explain the answer that you gave to this question. Please give that explanation now." And because the cross-examiner declined the request to allow the witness to explain, there should not be another chance to cross-examine based upon whatever the answer is.

The two main purposes of cross-examination are to get answers that advance the case of the cross-examiner and to get answers that detract from the case of the direct examiner. But things do not always go smoothly, regardless of preparation. If the witness says something in cross that advances the case of the direct examiner, this can be exploited in redirect. Once the door is open, the direct examiner can stress the point further on redirect.

If the answer appears to fit perfectly into the cross-examiner's plan, there is always the possibility of redirect upsetting the apple cart, as the examiner on redirect can still ask the witness to explain the answer. The cross-examiner may even have fallen into a trap set by the direct examiner, a trap that arises where the direct examiner chooses not to ask what appears to be the hard question, with the hope that the cross-examiner will ask it. This can have a major impact. In redirect, once the answer has been explained, there is no further cross-examination. The cross-examiner is now stuck with the answer.

Conclusion

THESE SITUATIONS ILLUSTRATE the risk-reward challenge of cross-examination. If the cross-examiner asks no questions, nothing will be accomplished. However, questions asked in cross-examination may cause more harm than good.

CASE STUDY

IN A WRONGFUL dismissal case, the manager who had dismissed the employee did not testify about a letter, which extolled the work performed by the employee, written by customer AB. The letter was produced in pre-trial disclosure but has not yet been identified in the trial.

Discuss the pros and cons of the following sequence of questions:

HEADLINE. I will now ask you about the plaintiff's performance in working with AB's file.

Q. The plaintiff did work for that client, correct?

A. Yes.

Q. And did that work well, correct?

A. . . .

Solution

PROS: In almost any dismissal case, the employee wants to establish that past performance was exemplary. A third-party endorsement goes a long way to support that. It puts the employer in a dilemma: whether to involve the client in the dispute and show that the work may not have been as good as represented. Go for it!

CONS: Beware the unknown. The employer knew that the letter was out there, yet counsel did not inoculate the manager against that obvious cross-examination sequence. Why not? The letter can be used to impeach anything negative that the manager says unless the manager has a zinger answer such as the following:

Q. And did that work well, correct?

A. Not so. The plaintiff rigged the contract, and we had to pay substantial damages to AB to make up for it.

Browne v Dunn

Browne v Dunn is a British rule of practice, adopted in several common law jurisdictions. It comes into play when a cross-examiner intends to lead evidence from another witness who is yet to testify to contradict what the current witness has to say. The cross-examiner must put that piece of evidence to the witness during the cross-examination. This avoids the requirement that the current witness re-attend afterward to explain the contradiction. The rule does not apply to what earlier witnesses have said. It is a rule of civility and efficiency that reduces inconvenience to the witness, invites the witness to explain what could be embarrassing evidence that will arise later, and avoids the judge's asking later, when the future witness testifies, "I wonder what the first witness would say about that?"

Browne v Dunn is a form of impeachment exercise. Instead of using an inconsistent statement previously made by the testifying witness, the examiner will use later testimony coming from a future witness as the contradictory statement. Here is the formula:

1. The cross-examiner confirms the current testimony, locking the witness into a position that the cross-examiner intends to attack.
2. Then the cross-examiner confronts the witness with what the future witness will say. Unlike impeachment, however, the cross-examiner MUST ask the current witness to accept, deny, or explain the difference. In impeachment, this is optional for the cross-examiner. Where possible, the cross-examiner should have the testifying witness identify the future witness and confirm the probity of that other witness's future testimony.
3. The cross-examiner must have the future witness available to testify at the appropriate time in the trial. This is discussed in greater detail below.

During cross-examination, the issue of which evidence to accept (this witness's or the future witness's) is a matter of comparative weight. How can the cross-examiner establish that the future witness's expected testimony carries more weight than that of the testifying witness? During cross-examination, the testifying witness should be called to account for weaknesses in that witness's testimony. At the same time, the testifying witness should be asked to support the appearance of strength in the future witness's testimony. The section "Relative Credibility —

Is Mine Better Than Yours?" above in Chapter 1, deals with this issue.

Whether the cross-examiner should continue the line of cross-examination after the conclusion of the impeachment remains a judgment call. Once the cross has established that the testifying witness differs from the future witness, the impeachment has been completed. However, the cross-examination could continue the subject with a view to suggesting the punchline "So you can't be sure that you are correct on that, can you?"

EXAMPLE

IN DIRECT EXAMINATION, the witness has testified that the car had been speeding through the intersection. The cross-examiner has another witness who will testify that the car had proceeded slowly through the intersection. The table is set for the application of the *Browne v Dunn* principle. This witness has said something, and another witness will say something different. Here is how the cross-examiner will apply the rule (the answer to each question will be "yes"):

HEADLINE. [CONFIRMATION] I will now ask you about the car as it entered the intersection.

Q. You saw the car approach the intersection, correct?

Q. You were standing at the northeast corner of the intersection, correct?

Q. The car approached from the south, correct?

Q. As I understand your testimony in chief, you said that the car was travelling quickly, correct?
Q. You said it was speeding, correct?
Q. That is, it was travelling faster than the speed limit, correct?

HEADLINE. [CONFRONTATION] I will now put to you what Ms Jones has to say.
Q. Were you aware that there was someone standing at the southeast corner of that intersection?
Q. Ms Jones will testify that she was standing at the southeast corner of that same intersection. She will testify that she had a clear line of sight to the car in question. You would agree that such a person would have a clear view of what transpired in the intersection, correct?
Q. Ms Jones will testify that the car approached from the south. You agree with that, correct?
Q. Ms Jones will testify that the car was travelling slowly. You have disagreed with that, correct?
Q. Ms Jones will testify that the car was travelling well below the speed limit. You disagreed with that, correct?
Q. Now, I suggest to you that Ms Jones is correct and that you are not correct in your recollection. What do you say about what Ms Jones has to say?

DISCUSSION

IT IS IMPERATIVE that the cross-examiner put to the witness a fair representation of what the future witness will say. If the future witness does not testify at all or says something that is materially different, the cross-examiner will have to explain this or face sanction from the trial judge. It is therefore imperative that the cross-examiner have the future witness under summons or subpoena, or can otherwise guarantee the attendance of the witness. If the current witness accedes to what the future witness will say, that attendance is no longer necessary. It is, however, a serious breach of ethics should the cross-examiner invent the testimony of that future witness.

In practice, counsel can comply with the formula described above quite simply. As the witness says something controversial, the cross-examiner can simply ask, "Well, Ms Jones says otherwise. What do you say about that?" A good practice is for the cross-examiner to separate the evidence of the future witness into several short statements, each consisting of one discrete fact, as in the example above. Then, if the witness disagrees with the overall statement, the cross-examiner can put each separate fact to the witness to accept or contest. This sets up the future witness's testimony.

Conclusion

BY ITSELF, THE *Browne v Dunn* principle is a matter of formula, with which counsel must comply to arrive at the desired conclusion. In practice, it can be a helpful way to focus the attention of the trial judge on the controversy, and from there, the cross-examiner will try to demonstrate the relative weakness of the current testimony.

CASE STUDY

IN A CASE involving the sale of a used car, the dealer who sold the three-year-old car told the purchaser and testifies in chief that the car had never been in an accident. The cross-examiner pulled up the records to learn that the car had been in an accident two years before, with a substantial insurance claim for damages to the car. The insurance adjuster, AB, will testify that the insurer paid off that earlier claim. AB is waiting outside the courtroom.

Create the headlines and questions to comply with *Browne v Dunn*.

Solution

HEADLINE. [CONFIRMATION] Let's discuss the history of this car.

Q. Your dealership owned the car, correct?

A. Yes.

Q. And offered it for sale to the plaintiff, correct?

A. Yes.

Q. The plaintiff asked whether it was in an accident before, correct?

A. Yes.

Q. You told the plaintiff it had not, correct?

A. Yes.

HEADLINE. [CONFRONTATION] I will now tell you what someone else has to say about the history of that car.

Q. I have an insurance adjuster, AB, outside this room. Do you know this adjuster?

A. I don't think so.

Q. AB will testify that he was employed by an insurer, CD, that insured this car two years before your dealership acquired it Would you agree that CD did in fact insure the car at that time?

A. How would I know?

Q. AB will further testify that this car was involved in an accident two years before your dealership acquired it, which accident was the subject of a claim brought by the former owner to CD. That statement is true, correct?

A. Again, my firm did not own the car at that time. We wouldn't know.

Q. AB will further testify that CD paid $10,000 on account of damages to this car following this accident. That statement is true, correct?

A. I doubt it.

Q. AB was the adjuster who handled the claim. That statement is also true, correct?

A. I don't know.

Q. Now, I put it to you that this very car was in an accident before you sold it to my client?

Impeachment

IMPEACHMENT DOES NOT arise in every cross-examination. Indeed, it does not arise in every trial. However, the most fun the trial lawyer will have is the successful impeachment of an opposition witness, which occurs when the witness says something at trial different from what the witness has said earlier. There is a specific choreography that applies to the impeachment process, and these are the dance steps. The lawyer has to follow each of the steps necessary to get from beginning to end:

1. Identify what the witness has to say today. This is called confirmation. The lawyer wants to make sure that the witness is saying something now that contradicts what was said before. This requires the lawyer to have the witness confirm exactly what the witness now says. Because the current testimony must conflict with the earlier statement, it is essential that the lawyer phrase the question in a manner that sets up the contradiction as starkly as possible: "Just to confirm, your evidence today is . . . ."
2. Once the lawyer has established that the witness has something contradictory to say in testimony, the lawyer must go back in time and identify the circumstances in which the witness made the earlier statement. This is referred to as the credit phase. The witness should be asked to establish the circumstances in which the earlier statement was given, and which should show that the witness intended to be truthful at that time. Examples follow below. Statements can be written or oral, and they can be given to a third party or recorded. Whether a statement was actually true or credible remains to be discussed.

- "Do you recall being examined for discovery on 3 August 2012? You were under oath to tell the truth, correct?"
- "You wrote a letter to the Admissions Department at the University of Toronto, correct? You knew that you had to be truthful in your communication with the university, correct?"
- "You attended at the Emergency Department of the Ottawa Hospital on 3 August 2012, correct? And you spoke to the admissions nurse, correct? You knew that your treatment depended on the accuracy of your disclosure, correct?"

3. The final step is the confrontation. The lawyer presents the statement to the witness as something said or written by the witness on the earlier occasion:
   - "I will now read to you from the transcript of your examination."
   - "I now produce a copy of that letter for your identification. Is this the letter? I will now read to you from the second paragraph."
   - "I am producing a copy of the emergency records from the Ottawa Hospital dated 3 August 2012. I will now read to you from the notes recorded by the emergency-room nurse."

In each case, the lawyer will confront the witness with what was said or recorded in the earlier circumstance. That is the impeachment, and that is the end of the exercise. What happens next is a judgment call.

In many cases, there is a fourth step, the commitment. In this step, the lawyer has the witness adopt one story or the other. Not only has the witness's credibility been shaken, but one of the elements of the lawyer's case is now supported by this witness. Does the lawyer want to rely upon the accuracy of the earlier statement? If so, the lawyer asks questions to establish that the circumstances of the earlier statement are more reliable than those of the current testimony. Does the lawyer want to rely upon the accuracy of the current testimony? If so, one wonders why the impeachment was appropriate in the first place. Nevertheless, if the purpose was to attack credibility, the lawyer asks questions to establish that the circumstances of the earlier statement are less reliable than those of the current testimony. Does the lawyer not care which of the two statements is accurate? If so, the lawyer will capitalize on the credibility problem that arises when the witness contradicts earlier statements.

Lawyers can use impeachment IF AND ONLY IF these factors apply:

- There must be an inconsistency. Impeachment cannot be used to refer to what the witness said earlier where that earlier statement was similar to what is being said now.
- The inconsistency must be material — it must matter. Purple versus mauve, a mile versus a kilometre, big versus midsize: these may not meet this standard.

Lawyers should be alert for obvious explanations for the difference, such as a simple slip-up, a misuse of words, or an inaccurate recording of the earlier statement.

The cross-examiner should leave hanging the implicit question, "Were you lying then or now?" The trial judge will be very interested in a successful impeachment, as it may form the turning point of the case. But if the lawyer sets up an impeachment and does not deliver, the lawyer's credibility with the judge will be harmed. Both conditions must be met — inconsistency and materiality.

Conclusion

IMPEACHMENT MUST BE thought out in advance because it is so easy to waste the opportunity when it arises. The exploitation of previous inconsistent statements is a matter of art. Finally, once the impeachment has been successful, the lawyer should not waste effort in a senseless set of questions that allows the witness to recover from the trap set by the impeachment.

CASE STUDY

IN A LIBEL case, the plaintiff, AB, says that the author of a letter to the editor of the local newspaper actually knew that the plaintiff had served in the army honourably, contrary to what was implied in the letter. The author testified in chief that there was no communication between the plaintiff and the author about the subject. The plaintiff has uncovered a letter dated earlier the same year sent by the author to a colleague, CD, which states, "AB and I discussed her overseas record. I don't believe what she says. She is lying to cover up her failure."

Identify the inconsistency (before, the witness said this, but now, the witness says this), and create a sequence of questions to impeach on that inconsistency. Should there be an effort to commit the witness to one position or the other?

Solution

BEFORE, THE WITNESS said there was a discussion about AB's overseas record. Now, the witness denies such a discussion.

Q. [CONFIRMATION] You did not discuss AB's overseas record with AB, correct?

Q. [CREDIT] You wrote to CD earlier the same year, correct? I am showing you that letter. You sent this to CD at that time, correct? And you signed it, correct? You were telling CD the truth, correct?

Q. [CONFRONTATION] I direct your attention to the third paragraph, which reads, "AB and I discussed her overseas record. I don't believe what she says. She is lying to cover up her failure." You wrote that, correct?

Judgment Calls in Cross-examination

CROSS-EXAMINATION OCCURS IN real time. The cross-examiner routinely receives answers that are not expected, and judges offer unexpected input. What does the cross-examiner do then? These are the judgment calls that test the skill of the cross-examiner. There are other judgment calls discussed elsewhere in this handbook. Almost every section refers to at least one.

Is it the question too many?

THE MOST COMMON judgment call is whether to ask the dreaded possible question too many. Usually, this question arises after answers are given that appear to lead to one conclusion, which is a conclusion that the cross-examiner wants to draw. Should the cross-examiner leave it alone, or should the answer be rubbed in the face of the witness? "So, in light of those answers, how can you say . . ."

Here is the risk. If the cross-examiner asks the question, then the answer may be devastating — to the cross-examiner. Just because the cross-examiner cannot imagine a reconciliation between two contradictory answers, this does not mean that the witness cannot explain, and worse, the explanation may be convincing.

When the cross-examiner is not sure that the audience gets the point, there is a tendency to ask the extra question, to make the extra effort to nail down the point. If the judge is new to the area of practice, it may be that the cross-examiner has to make that extra effort. If the point is crucial to the evidence, then the judgment call becomes all the more serious.

Impeachment

IN IMPEACHMENT, THERE are often two judgment calls that arise. First, is the point material enough to start the impeachment exercise? Remember that the trial judge will be on high alert when the impeachment formula begins, and the judge will take it out on the lawyer if the exercise fails to lead to a significant result. Second, should the cross-examiner have the witness choose one of the two conflicting stories? This choice arises immediately after the confrontation phase. The point is now made: the witness said something before that is different from what is being said now. So what? The obvious issue is whether or not to continue the sequence of questions to establish that the position the cross-examiner prefers is the more credible. But what if neither is preferable?

Follow-ups to unexpected answers

THE ANSWER GIVEN by a witness may invite further questions. If the cross-examiner is not prepared for those further questions, it will be a judgment call whether to ask them. There may be a very good reason not to do so, which escapes the cross-examiner while in full stride. Perhaps a five-minute break will assist the cross-examiner in weighing the options.

The semi-adversarial witness

IS THE WITNESS adversarial? On this specific testimony? There are witnesses who are truly independent, and it becomes a judgment call whether to exploit the opportunity to cross-examine aggressively. It may be that the cross-examiner wants to ask open questions, or soft leading questions, to bring out the story from the witness. Some witnesses are both adversarial in some respects and non-adversarial in others. In these circumstances, cross-examiners should not be over-aggressive as aggression causes defensive behaviour by the witness, which can be harmful to the cross-examiner's case.

Leaving the confines of the outline

WHETHER THE LAWYER should go off-script is a common judgment call. The safe strategy is to follow the outline. However, the outline may not be the best strategy in light of the actual testimony in chief, answers given earlier in the cross, or comments from the trial judge. Sometimes, the trial lawyer just has a sense that things are not proceeding as expected. Does the lawyer follow the gut instinct? Experience will show the lawyer whether or not to trust those sensations.

Objections

OBJECTIONS INVOLVE JUDGMENT calls, both when to make them and how to respond. While the cross-examination is in full flight, it is a distraction to argue an objection, and often the path of least resistance is for the cross-examiner to rephrase and go on. But sometimes the answer is important — important enough to stand and contest the objection, and sometimes there is a pattern of objection that itself calls for a response. Tactical objections deserve censure by the trial judge. Should the cross-examiner seek this protection?

Whether to stay seated

ONE OF THE basic judgment calls that lawyers have to make is whether to cross-examine the witness at all. Lawyers do not have to rise and ask questions — they can decline the opportunity. Essentially, the lawyer has to have a point to make, and the following questions can help assess the risk-to-reward ratio:

- What risks arise from trying to make the point?
- How likely can the point be made?
- How important is the point in the first place?
- Where does the point fit in the case analysis?

Conclusion

CASE ANALYSIS IS what guides all cross-examination decisions. The elements of the case have to be proved or, when considering the opposition, disproved. How does this witness help or hurt one side or the other? If the witness did not harm the cross-examiner's case in direct examination, why attack credibility? In fact, why cross-examine at all?

As with many other things in litigation, junior lawyers have to make judgment calls on the fly with which they have little experience. Then they have to live with the decision, for good or for ill. They should make the best call that they can, and get on with things, not dwelling on the past, as this may infect their decisions in the future.

The Sympathetic Witness in Cross-examination

ONE OF THE more difficult tactical situations for the cross-examiner is the sympathetic witness, who has suffered, is aged, is young, or is disabled. This witness cries out for the sympathy of the audience. How is this witness to be cross-examined?

Basic case analysis sets the table. Just as with any other witness, the cross-examiner must decide what is to be accomplished with the cross-examination of this witness. How can this witness either help or hurt, and what is to be done about credibility? Just as important as case analysis are theme and back story. Recall that the theme of the trial attempts to establish why the direct examiner's or cross-examiner's position should prevail. The sympathetic witness represents a major obstacle because the cross-examiner wants to establish the evidence that will support or damage the relevant elements of case analysis without sacrificing the theme and back story and without preparation with the witness beforehand — a delicate operation indeed.

Once it has been decided what is to be accomplished, the next question is how to approach the cross-examination itself. The greater the level of sympathy toward the witness, the greater the degree of tact that is required by the examiner. The cross-examiner must be very careful to appear gentle. This requires that the cross-examiner use a softer voice, that the pace of speech be slower, and that the use of language be more gentle — less confrontational, but not so far as to appear patronizing or smarmy. Naturally kind: that's the ticket.

This does not mean that the questions themselves must be gentle. Hard questions may be asked of all witnesses, regardless of the sympathy they draw. Even the young child and the war veteran suffering from post-traumatic stress disorder may be asked hard questions — hard questions asked gently. The risk that the cross-examiner faces is that the appearance of bullying will negate any benefit accomplished by the testimony. It is a pyrrhic victory indeed for the cross-examiner to achieve a technical success but lose favour with the audience. The formula for success with the sympathetic witness is, in fact, no different than with any other witness — headlines, short questions, simple language — just add a new element — kindness.

The outline requires more creativity. How can these questions be phrased so that the judge and the witness are not offended? More so than with other witnesses, the cross-examiner does not want to provoke an argument with the sympathetic witness. Guess who usually wins that argument? The questions may be similar to those posed to any witness, sympathetic or not. Just add the appropriate use of tone, pace, and gentle language, and the result should be acceptable.

Conclusion

IF THE CROSS-EXAMINER is guided by common decency, it is likely that the questioning can be toned down to an appropriate level. This will make the cross-examiner part of the team that tries to get to the truth, and usually the trial judge will respect the lawyer who tries to act in an appropriate manner.

The Unsympathetic Witness in Cross-examination

IF THE SYMPATHETIC witness pulls on the heartstrings of the trial judge, what about the unsympathetic witness? Does cross-examination of this witness become a piece of cake? Not so. This witness may come with some obvious baggage, but beware that the attributes that make this witness unsympathetic may also affect the emotions of the cross-examiner. Angry cross-examiners are rarely successful ones. Consider the role Al Pacino played in the 1979 film *. . . And Justice for All*, a classic portrayal of an over-the-top litigator, emotionally out of control.

Here are some important tips to remember when cross-examining the unsympathetic witness:

- The cross-examiner should keep cool. Emotions should not govern the cross-examination — ever. If emotions are taking control, it is time for a fifteen-minute recess.
- The cross-examiner may deliver the questions in a flat or wooden tone of voice, devoid of emotion. Contrast this technique to the gentleness required for the cross-examination of the sympathetic witness.
- It is the testimony of the witness that counts. If the lawyer does feel the impact of emotions, the lawyer should retreat to the usual formula: headlines, short questions, simple language. Add a possible "deadpan delivery" to the list.
- Perhaps more so than with other witnesses, the cross-examiner should slow down. The idea is to let the unsympathetic witness behave unsympathetically.
- If the reason for the lack of sympathy arises from the witness's testimony, the cross-examination should not undo the positive effect already accomplished. Avoid the extra questions if their efficacy is in doubt.
- If the reason for the lack of sympathy arises from the witness's conduct (on the stand or in the events

that led to the case), this conduct should be presented to the witness to acknowledge. This may be difficult under the rules of evidence if the conduct is not relevant to the issues, and it may be necessary for legal research to uncover some basis on which this evidence becomes admissible.

Sympathy or the lack thereof plays to the theme and back story. In both cases, the cross-examiner wants to establish why the case for which the witness was called should not prevail. This should be accented by the cross-examination.

Conclusion

THE CROSS-EXAMINATION OF an unsympathetic witness can do more harm than good. The last thing that the cross-examiner wants is to make the unsympathetic witness neutral or, worse, sympathetic. Getting into an argument with the unsympathetic witness may put the witness into the position of victim — not a good result.

When the Judge Takes Over the Cross-examination

DURING CROSS-EXAMINATION, THE lawyer should be in total control of what goes on. Subject to stepping over the line with improper questions, counsel should be able to pursue any relevant line of inquiry. What happens when the judge interferes, hijacking the cross-examination? Judges are not supposed to take over any examination where there are competent lawyers. In the adversarial system, judges are supposed to trust counsel to do the job right. For the most part, trial judges only introduce a new line of question after both direct and cross are completed, and when they do this, they usually offer both lawyers the opportunity for further examination (direct or cross) with respect to anything that arose during the judge's inquiry. At least, that is the convention.

Judges intervene when one of two things occurs:

1. When a witness has not been allowed the opportunity to explain. Often, the judge will interrupt the cross-examination and direct the witness to give a full answer. True, the leading question may have properly demanded a "yes" or "no" answer, but nevertheless the trial judge wants to hear what the witness has to say. If that occurs, there is nothing that the cross-examiner can do about it. Clearly, this trial judge wants to let the witness testify in full. The cross-examiner should take this into account should the opportunity arise later, and then when the witness has something to offer in addition to "yes" or "no," the lawyer should invite it.
2. When the trial judge wants to pursue a specific line of inquiry not covered by the cross. This interest by the judge is very important information that the cross-examiner wants to know. What does the trial judge want to learn? Anything that motivates the trial judge should interest the cross-examiner.

One difficulty that arises from judicial intervention is that the cross-examiner cannot take the time necessary to prepare the next line of questions, to follow up what the judge has asked. Worse, the judge may put the lawyer's plan of action out of sequence. In that case, it is acceptable for the lawyer to interrupt the trial judge with the remark "May it please the court, but I was getting to that line of inquiry. May I do so in my own sequence?"

Perhaps the line of inquiry is dramatically different from what was planned. If so, it is acceptable for the cross-examiner to ask for a brief recess after the judge's questions to consider how to deal with what the judge has asked. The important thing to remember is that this is an area the trial judge wants to learn about. The cross-examiner must find a way to plug that information into the plans for that witness and for the case. How does this fit into the case analysis? The direct examiner may still have the opportunity to deal with the subject in redirect, and if that happens, there may be no opportunity for further cross-examination on the subject.

The judge's questions and the witness's answers open up areas for both lawyers to explore further. Is the direct examiner limited to non-leading questions? Yes. And both lawyers are limited to what emerged from the judge's inquiry. That said, most judges allow lawyers to ask questions arising from answers to the lawyers' further questions. Occasionally, this creates a full sequence of "redirect" and "recross," and while it seems that this may become a never-ending process, it is rare and usually quite brief.

An unusual circumstance may arise where the trial judge asks for inadmissible evidence during the interruption. In that case, the cross-examiner should take a strong stand and make an objection, as it is quite possible that the trial judge did not consider the admissibility when launching into the inquiry. But the trial judge may well overrule the objection. At the very least, the cross-examiner will have the opportunity to ask further questions.

Conclusion

THE TRIAL JUDGE is looking for information and, in doing so, alerting the cross-examiner to what interests the judge. This information is vitally important to the trial lawyer. It should be a guide for cross-examination and may well inform the final argument.

When to Ask If You Don't Know the Answer

JUNIOR LITIGATORS ARE often told never to ask a question to which they don't know the answer. This advice usually comes from lawyers who do not litigate. Litigators often ask questions to which they don't know the answer. In chief, they get to practise, to rehearse, and to try out these questions, but in cross-examination, they do not. This invites the question, when should litigators leap into the unknown?

There are at least three separate situations when it is appropriate to ask the question to which the cross-examiner does not have the answer:

1. Early in the cross-examination, the cross-examiner may be operating in "friendly" mode and want to draw evidence from the witness for use later in the cross-examination. Or perhaps the witness is being friendly and is providing testimony that assists the cross-examiner's case. In these circumstances, asking a question to which the answer is unknown may in-

volve an acceptable risk. If the answer comes back unfavourably, the cross-examiner still has the time to recover with targeted leading questions that attack or reshape the answer. In this case, the attack questions should lead in the direction where the cross-examiner does know all the answers.

2. The cross-examiner can probe into unknown territory where the answers are not likely to cause any harm. They may serve as background, or they may be in response to closed either/or questions to which one or both of the possible answers are acceptable.
3. Then there is the "Hail Mary pass," referring to Doug Flutie's desperate winning play for the Boston College Eagles football team in 1984: The case is lost if the question does not have an answer that is favourable, just as the Eagles would have gone on to lose to the University of Miami Hurricanes but for a successful touchdown pass in the dying moments of the game. This may be a circumstance of desperation, and it is unusual for the cross-examiner to be put in this position, but it does occur. Typically, for this to work, the witness should be relatively independent, even though called by the opposition. The cross-examiner genuinely does not know the answer — in other words, the cross-examiner throws the dice when they are not loaded against the cross-examiner's client.

It is common for the cross-examiner to put to the witness a question to which an unfavourable answer is expected. This is the circumstance of *Browne v Dunn*, discussed above in this chapter. It is also the circumstance of the cross-examiner dealing with the opposing party on the witness stand. Basically, some questions just have to be asked, and the cross-examiner already knows the answers. They are unfavourable. What is rare is the leap into the unknown when in attack mode of cross-examination. A five-and-out sequence in cross will likely fail if the witness answers outside the expectation and if the lawyer lacks the evidence with which to impeach.

Conclusion

THIS IS ANOTHER circumstance in which a cross-examiner must make a judgment call in real time. The admonition not to ask the question is only a warning. A judgment call is coming up! Pay attention and tread carefully!

When to Stop Asking Questions in Cross-examination

FAR TOO OFTEN, lawyers continue to ask questions after they have accomplished all that they can reasonably expect, as if they like to hear the sound of their own voice. Maybe it is a control thing. How does the cross-examiner know when it is time to sit down?

Start with the case analysis. What is it that the cross-examiner expects to accomplish with this witness? How does the cross assist the case, harm the opposition's case, or influence credibility in the desired direction? But that is only the first half of the determination. The other half is found in the balance between risk and reward.

Every question asked in cross-examination involves some risk. The adversarial witness will use every opportunity to defeat the cross-examiner, and every question gives the witness another opportunity to do so. The cross-examination consists of a series of points, with each point involving some level of risk. The cross-examiner can evaluate whether the risk is increasing or decreasing as the cross goes on. In perfect courtroom choreography, the cross-examiner would sit after an especially dramatic point is made. Dream on! That happens on television. In real life, the cross-examiner usually asks the stunning, dramatic question and gets pie in the face.

The outline prepared by the cross-examiner in the preparation phase calls for a sequence of questions, which is a logical progression from the beginning to the end of the cross-examination. Deviation often occurs during the cross in the following circumstances:

- The cross-examiner will deviate from the plan to adjust for the answers being given, taking a different approach altogether. This is most common with a witness whose direct testimony is very brief or unexpectedly harmless.
- The cross-examiner may insert points as opportunities arise from the direct examination, just completed.
- The cross-examiner may adjust the sequence to account for what has already occurred in the cross.
- Any intervention by the trial judge, whether in chief or cross, will prompt the lawyer to rethink the outline decisions.

All of these adjustments will affect the cross-examiner's decision when to sit down. Has the examination accomplished all that could reasonably be expected? If so, sit down. Will the next point involve too great a level of risk? If so, sit down. Has the trial judge given an indication that the cross has gone on too long? If so, consider sitting down, but just because the judge thinks nothing more will be accomplished, this does not make it so. The lawyer remains in control. What comes next had better be good, though. Immediately before sitting down, the cross-examiner should request a few moments to gather thoughts: "I just have to review my notes, Your Honour. I may be finished, but I want to be certain." The trial judge will grant this request almost every time.

Know Yourself as a Cross-examiner

EACH LAWYER BRINGS to the practice of law different attributes and skills. For the litigator to be comfortable practising law, the tactics and behaviours of practice must be aligned with that litigator's abilities and character. Young lawyers often do not consider this until it is too late to change course.

There are various ways to measure personal attributes:

- Are you more or less aggressive?
- Are you more or less self-confident?
- How about your willingness to take risks?
- Are you sensitive or squeamish about some subjects?
- Do you speak loudly, quickly, or both?
- Are you quick to anger?
- Do you judge others?
- Do you detest being judged by others?

- How well can you take criticism?
- Does competition bring out the best or the worst in you?

Any style of cross-examination must take the attributes of the lawyer into account. Witnesses, opposing counsel, and judges can all sense when other lawyers act outside of their natural character. It will appear unnatural for a passive person to act aggressively, and vice versa. That said, it is the words that matter. An aggressive cross-examination can still be conducted with a soft voice and words spoken slowly. It may take time and practice to discover the natural character of the cross-examiner, especially with young lawyers who do not have much experience in or out of the courtroom.

Input from colleagues or more senior counsel can be of assistance, and mentorship, when available, can be very important here. A lawyer who acts out of character may have difficulty sleeping or develop an alcohol or medication dependency. This symptom of vulnerability is not a subject to raise with opposing counsel at a confrontational meeting. If the young lawyer practises in a firm, it may be helpful to have a senior colleague attend a court session, and after the session, the young lawyer can ask for guidance or advice. While nothing serves as a good substitute for the real thing, practice in front of a video camera can prove enlightening. Many continuing education opportunities allow for video recording of practice sessions.

Conclusion

AN EFFECTIVE CROSS-EXAMINATION can be exhilarating for the lawyer who conducts it, and an ineffective one can be very disheartening. Virtually every case exposes the trial lawyer to both ups and downs. If lawyers act outside of their natural character, the stress of this volatility can make the practice of advocacy very unrewarding in the long term.

chapter six

Redirect Examinations

SENIOR LITIGATORS MAY have to think long and hard about the last time that they conducted a successful redirect examination. In theory, no question can be asked in a redirect that does not start with the words "In cross-examination, you testified that . . . ." The purpose of redirect is to clear up any confusion or ambiguity that arose during the cross-examination. This often takes the form of counsel's putting to the witness a question that the witness was not given the opportunity to answer in the cross-examination. For example, take a witness who answered a question asking for a "yes" or "no" answer with the words "May I explain?" Or perhaps the witness's answer was cut short by another question. Assuming that the trial judge did not intervene and request that the witness explain or complete the answer, it is up to the direct examiner to put that request to the witness in redirect:

- "In cross-examination, you tried to explain your affirmative answer to this question. Would you please provide that explanation now?"

- "In cross-examination, you started to answer this question. Would you please complete that answer now?"

The concept of "splitting your case" comes from the idea that there are issues the opposition can raise that should be anticipated by the examiner. For example, if a case involves liability and damages, the direct examination should not be restricted to liability where it is foreseeable that the witness will be cross-examined on damages. The direct examiner should elicit testimony about both those issues. The questions cannot simply wait until redirect.

EXAMPLE

THE PLAINTIFF HAS made a claim for costs to complete a construction project. The defendant not only denies responsibility for those extra costs but has claimed that the plaintiff overcharged and delayed the project and that these overcharges and delays cost the defendant money, for which the defendant counterclaims. The witness is an engineer who knows about the completion of the project as well as the time it should have taken to complete. During the direct examination of the engineer, counsel who called the witness should elicit evidence on both subjects. The trial judge will likely not permit a full discussion of the delay-claim issues in redirect.

The reason why so few redirects stand out as successes is that direct examiners do not know what their witnesses will say. Usually, they do not practise this because if they had, there would have been a sequence of questions to cover the subject in the direct examination. Lawyers dislike asking questions in new areas because of the risks involved. Before the lawyer asks redirect questions, consideration should be given to whether something positive can result from the redirect. If so, what are the risks? Reward versus risk — the usual judgment call of trial counsel.

Conclusion

WHEN LAWYERS PREPARE the outline for the direct examination of witnesses, they should anticipate all of the issues that opposing counsel will raise. If these are reflected in the pleadings, they should be fully canvassed during the direct testimony. Lawyers can only raise subjects in redirect that both were raised in cross-examination and could not reasonably have been anticipated from the pleadings.

CASE STUDY

IN A DEBT default case, the borrower claims that the bank manager promised to allow adequate time for the borrower to close a transaction that would have seen the bank repaid. In cross-examination, the following exchange occurs with the borrower:

Q1. You said that you asked for more time, correct?
  A. Yes, I did.
Q2. To close this transaction with AB, correct?
  A. Yes, that's right.

Q3. But the deal was not binding yet, was it?

A. Well, it was a handshake deal. [PAUSE]

Q4. But not enforceable, right?

A. Well, I thought so.

Q5. Not in writing, right?

A. Not yet.

Assuming that this ends the exchange and that counsel moves on to other areas, how can the redirect examination allow the witness to explain? Create a headline and a few open questions to do so.

Solution

HEADLINE. During cross-examination, you were asked about your pending deal with AB. You said it was a "handshake deal."

Q. What did you mean by that?

Q. How could you rely on AB to close the deal?

Q. What did you tell the banker about that?

Conclusion

THERE ARE SEVERAL themes that form the basis of this handbook, and indeed all of the handbooks in the Young Advocates Series:

1. Foremost is that the advocate should consider the other participants, who all have roles to play and who all have other things on their mind. For lawyers to be successful, they should accommodate as many of these competing interests as possible. They should only pick fights that they can win. Even so, a fight avoided is usually better than a fight engaged in and won.
2. This theme is found in the title of the section "Short Questions, Simple Language," above in Chapter 1. To be effective, lawyers must communicate. The longer the sentence and the more complicated the language, the less effective is that communication.
3. Inexperienced counsel should identify good practices and avoid bad ones. Many of these techniques can be reduced to simple formulas, such as "headline and five-and-out."

4. Lawyers have a strategic advantage over many other members of society: their ability to manipulate words to accomplish a goal. But this requires that lawyers consider the goal before they speak, and many do not. A sports team that is given control of the ball should relinquish that control reluctantly. The inherent advantage of being the one who guides the conversation can be squandered with aimless questions, as control of the discussion quickly passes to the witness.

As with all of the handbooks in the Young Advocates Series, years of practical experience have led to the techniques that are presented here. All have been presented in the Advocacy Club. The techniques work, though they may not be perfect, and they may not be ideal. However, they work. For the junior litigator, these techniques are essential to unlocking the creativity that will lead to the best result.

The solutions proposed in this handbook can be controversial. They do not represent a one-size-fits-all solution, and they may not apply to all counsel. They may not apply to all situations. The question is whether this solution applies to this lawyer in this situation. If a young lawyer recognizes an issue, then that lawyer can make an informed decision as to the best method to resolve the issue. But the lawyer cannot make such an informed decision without that recognition. So here is the last kernel of wisdom to be imparted in this handbook: Think before you speak. What you say has consequences.

Index

About the Author

JOHN HOLLANDER RECEIVED his LLB from Queen's University in 1976 and was called to the Ontario bar in 1978. He is a practising lawyer with more than thirty-three years' experience as a civil trial advocate. He has a passion for mentoring and teaching young lawyers. He offers innovative seminars and workshops on both interview skills and advocacy. He currently teaches advanced trial advocacy at the University of Ottawa's Faculty of Law, Common Law Section.

Printed and bound by CPI Group (UK) Ltd, Croydon, CR0 4YY

30/06/2026

14910916-0001